How to Buy a Car:

Dealership "Secrets" Revealed

25 Year General Manager Reveals "Hidden Dealer Profits"
and Shows Proven Strategies to:

Save Thousands!

By

Jackson Jones

Table of Contents

Preface

What You Are Up Against

Have you ever been in a casino? You know, you walk in and lights and bells and whistles are going off everywhere, in front of you in strategically located places are games and activities of every type, all with one goal in mind, **to separate you from your money!** That's what today's dealerships are like. They are just like casinos.

From the moment you walk in, you are strategically lead to certain areas where people a lot smarter than you and I, have predetermined what would produce the best most effective and efficient environment to sell you a car.

Even the modern desks of today's dealerships are shaped with round edges, not square ones so that you feel like you are sitting around the desk not across which would present an adversarial environment and take away from the relaxed and comforting experience.

There are large flat screen TVs strategically located for your viewing pleasure, a play room to occupy your kids, with games and video screens so that you cannot be distracted while you are making a deal. Food is often being prepared so that you can eat and your kids can play **so there is no reason to leave without making a deal.**

All the new dealership designs are customer friendly. I worked for an import manufacturer that made us remodel our dealership to their new strict standards. The receptionist desk is located as soon as you enter the store so she can alert the sales manager when a customer is leaving without their knowledge. Specific lighting is installed to highlight the cars on certain glossy tile floors with warm colors and special paint to keep you relaxed and interested.

Today's salesperson is highly trained and micro-managed by processes and procedures that are designed to control and manipulate you into their method of success. And what is the success they are searching for?

Yes to sell you a car, but not only to sell you a car, **but to make the most profit imaginable** and hope for a perfect survey from you sent to the manufacturer. We will get into the importance that survey later.

How does all this end up? You get swept up in the new car smell, get what you think is great money for your trade, get the payments that you want at the interest rate you think is fair, which leaves room for some extra products like gap insurance and an extended warranty, and leave a happy camper.

What really happened? **You just overpaid for the car you bought,** agreed to far less than your trade was worth, accepted payments that could have been considerably lower, paid a higher interest rate than you qualified for and bought extra warranties and insurance **that put more profit in the dealer's pocket.**

You drive away happy while the sales manager and the sales person are giving each other a "high five" because **the dealership just made $6000 profit on your happy purchase** and you will **still** be sending in that perfect factory survey!

So let's begin our voyage into how all this works. The first thing that must happens is **the dealer must get you into the dealership,** they know nothing happens until you actually come to the dealership, they can't sell you a car over the phone or on the internet, you have to come in to do business so let's start with how they get you in.

Chapter 1

Dealer Advertising Tricks & Gimmicks

The first thing you must understand is that all dealer advertising be it print, direct mail, television or internet is designed to do one thing and one thing only....

"TO GET YOU INTO THE DEALERSHIP."

The dealer knows he cannot sell you a car over the phone or by email. He can entice you, or he can get you interested, but to actually sell you a car he must get you into the dealership to get you to sign on the "line that is dotted". **That is the motivating factor behind all dealership advertising.**

They will literally say anything possible to get you into the dealership such as...Zero Money Down, Zero Percent Financing, Thousands of dollars more for your trade than it's worth, no payments for six months, all credit accepted, up to 10,000 dollars off, thousands in rebates, lifetime warranties, free oil changes for life..."buy one car another car free"!, We will pay off your trade no matter what you owe! Heard these before?

So what do all these offers mean and are they for real? Well let's take a look.

2.

My experience has proven that by and large most dealers make these claims and some of them are legitimate. **But the majority of the time they are only designed to get you into the dealership.** Just like the casinos that offer all the perks and freebees to get you into their doors because they know the mathematical truth…**the house always wins!**

Zero Down. This is an effective and reliable offer from dealers and manufacturers to get you into the dealership by offering to sell you a car with no money down. Is it real? Absolutely, but it's not a offer that has any real value as people buy cars every day with little or no money down. On average most customers don't have any extra cash lying around to put down on a car, so to offer it in advertising costs nothing to the dealer.

He knows you probably don't have any money to put down any way, however most customers are embarrassed to admit they don't have any money for a down payment so when they read it in an advertisement they go in and use it without feeling embarrassed or belittled.

Anyone, based on the income they have and type of car they are trying to buy, can purchase a car with no money down. When you get there they will try to tell you that most lenders require 20% down **but that's not true**. The dealer knows that the amount of cash you have to put down usually equals extra profit to the dealer. We will cover this later.

3.

Zero Percent Financing. This is offered by dealers and by the manufacturers as an incentive to come in and finance a car with no finance charges. Is it real? Yes. You can absolutely finance a car at zero percent **IF** you and the car qualify with the factory.

Here is how it works. Let's say that ABC manufacturer wants to move the slow selling ABC crossover SUV. He will offer zero percent financing to buyers only on those units…they don't tell you that until you get to the dealership, so if you actually want another car, you may not get the zero percent.

They also don't tell you that you only get the zero percent if you finance for a short term only, usually like 36 to 48 months. You also have to have an exceptionally high credit score to qualify. But yes its free financing. **You also have to give up any cash rebates or incentives that would come with the car, you won't get both.**

I worked for a top 3 import manufacturer that would offer the zero percent on select models not only to move unpopular units, but also because they have done a study that shows that a larger percent of existing customers will buy from them again if they finance the car with their financing instead of paying cash.

The dealer likes it because now they are a lot more likely to sell you all the other products they offer in the finance or "business office" because you can simply add them into your payments rather than paying cash for them separately. For instance, the dealer extended warranty is around $1895.00.

But doesn't it sound better to say it's only $20 more dollars per month when you finance the car? If you pay cash and don't finance with the dealer, he has a harder time convincing you to scratch off a check for an additional amount of extras like warranties, gap insurance etc.

Thousands more for your trade than it's worth. Many advertisements will offer up to $3000 over Kelly Blue Book for you trade. The key words are those two little words "up to". That slipped right by you didn't it? That means they have the flexibility to offer you anything they want to for your trade "up to" the highest amount. **In my experience it is hardly ever offered.**

Again, you must remember that all they want to do is get you into the dealership. They know that if they offer you a ridiculous amount for your trade you are less likely to shop other dealers because of the amount. Here is what usually happens.

Your car is appraised and given an "ACV" or "actual cash value". (We will cover your trade allowance in more detail later), then whatever rebates are available and discounts off the car you want (assuming it's a new car) are all added to what your car is really worth to show a **inflated trade-in allowance**.

Or they simply show you in the fine print of the ad that nobody will or can read, that the trade- in amount is valued at dealership discretion, and based on a deduction for miles and overall condition. This is called "de-valuing" the trade. And it's done every day. Again, some customers agree to less for the trade and some don't. But it served its purpose, to get you into the dealership.

No payments from 90 days to Six Months. Again this is a real offer but **the customer pays for it**. Most car installment loans don't have the first payment due for 45 days. The dealer simply pays the finance institution a fee to extend that out so that they can offer it to you as an incentive to buy a car. I have rarely seen a customer get no payments for 6 months. Most of the time you have to have a perfect credit score which most people do not, and get the lender to approve to extend out the first payment that long. I said earlier the customer pays for doing it.

This is how they get you to pay for this amazing offer. Let's say it costs the dealer $400 to get the lender to extend your first payment. The dealer would know this upfront and simply under allow on your trade by $400 to off-set the expense.

So you got the extension **but you paid for it**. Also the interest accumulates differently when you extend your first payment out that long which can make your payment go up, so it's really not an advantage.

All credit applications accepted. Think of what this is saying. Yes, no matter how bad your credit is they will let you fill out a credit application and they will **accept it** so they can pull your credit to see your score. It doesn't mean you are approved they said "accepted" it's a slick play on words that looks like everyone is approved when in fact all they do is check your credit. A lot of credit challenged people fall for this all the time and run into the dealership.

Remember every time, you have a dealer check your credit, they send your application to at least 7 to 10 banks seeking approval. If you go to several dealerships in one day that could equal 30 inquires on your credit report and **drop your credit score.**

(More on credit and scores later). The only way a new car dealer can actually "accept" your credit is by getting a bank or lender to approve your loan.

Generally people that know they have credit issues or have been turned down by dealership financing before will "jump at the all credit applications accepted" ads. Remember, **accepted is not approved.**

The $199 a month Payment. Let's take a minute and distinguish between advertising that comes from the factory or manufacturer, typically done nationally on radio and TV and the local dealership that actually sells and services the car. Both are forms of advertising designed to get you into the local dealership, the only difference is that the factory doesn't care what dealer you buy their car from because they have already been paid for the car.

The dealer that orders the car from the factory pays for the car before it is even built, so the factory has their money, where as the local dealer wants you to buy it from them so they can recoup their money.

No doubt you have seen a cool car commercial on TV and after showing all the great things the car will do, they end up with "and now till Monday night get this amazing new car for only $199 a month! See local dealer for details.

Here's what you don't see. First off the car they showed with all the bells and whistles IS NOT the car they used to figure the $199 a month payment!

If you freeze your TV and could read the extremely small print at the bottom of the ad called the "disclosure" you will see it says "vehicle shown for illustration purposes only" that means that **the car you actually saw is much more expensive** and the car that qualifies for the S199 payment per month is stripped out with nothing but the basic equipment.

Also in the disclosure print you will see that **the payment quoted does not include tax, tag, title fees, dealer fees, and typically $2995 in cash down or trade equity.** This means that you must come out of pocket with around $4500 to $5000 down on a base car you don't really want to get to the $199 payment per month.

The factory ads typically are notorious for this deceptive advertising and this puts the pressure on the local dealer to handle all the unhappy customers that come in to get the deal. The local dealer is left to take the "heat". But you can do the math…$199 a month for a typical term of say 60 months is $12,000. How are you going to get that payment on a $20,000 plus vehicle?

I could advertise a $25,000 car for $59 a month simply by putting the required down payment in the disclosure box at the bottom of the screen. Nobody reads the disclosure, and it's only on the screen for a couple of seconds. Watch for this the next time you see a car commercial, how small the print is at the bottom, and how long it says on the screen. Good luck.

You can own this brand new loaded car for just $7995!
This too is deceptive advertising and you being a smart savvy consumer should know you can't a car that is

Another advertisement used a lot these days is the up to $10,000 off MSRP. This sounds great doesn't it? $10,000 off dealer MSRP? Most customers don't know what MSRP is. It stands for Manufacturers Suggested Retail Price. This price is the price set by the factory and placed on the window sticker as to what the dealer should try and sell the car for.

The problem with this advertising is if you look in the fine print, you will see the acronym MSRP stands for Manufactures Suggested Retail "PROFIT". Not PRICE, but PROFIT.

That means the dealer can over charge for his car as much as he wants to, and **any discount comes out of his profit. Again, it's a play on words.** The car business has become so competitive it's sad to see what dealers will do to sell a car.

We could go on and on with all the different dealership advertising that is out there, but I think you get the picture, dealership or factory ads are all designed To GET YOU IN THE DEALERSHIP.

No matter what they have to say or offer, if you come into the dealership they have all the math and numbers predetermined to sell you a car. Just like the casino, they know that selling cars is simply a "numbers game" **if they see enough customers a certain percentage will buy a car.**

I have seen customers ride up on a bicycle with no plans or means to buy a car, just to get the free "cruise tickets" or claim their flat screen TV or Ipad. And sure enough one of them leaves in a car!

"The national closing rate is about 25% of the customers that actually come on the lot". Dealerships do all the training and reports so that the math works out to their favor. If the average dealer wants to sell 5 cars a day, then they need to have 25 customers a day come on the lot.

Everything they do regarding advertising whether it is TV, newspaper, radio, direct mail or internet is designed to get the required number of people a day thru the door. And if they have the proper processes, people and procedures in place they will hit their number.

A customer on the lot is called an "up". Some dealerships have an open floor policy which means any salesperson can catch any customer, or a rotation system that means whichever salesperson is next on the list can catch the next available customer. **So when you come on the lot everything is planned and pre- determined to sell you a car.** Nothing happens by chance.

Chapter 2

Your Arrival

So let's say you've arrived on the lot due to some amazing offer you have seen, or simply because this is the local dealer that sells the car or truck or SUV you are looking for.

First off, remember as I said before, "nothing happens by chance" when you first arrive, you are only able to park in designated parking spaces.

This is by design, first you are forced to drive by or park next to vehicles that have been strategically placed there for various reasons.

Either they are "hit cars" which means they have been on the lot too long and need to go away, or they have enormous markup on the price placed on them to make a lot of profit or what is called "gross" in the car business.

Salespeople are alerted daily to these cars, and even given extra incentives to sell these cars. So once you have parked most dealerships have salespeople standing either outside or looking out the front windows and quickly approach you.

They are taught to speak to a customer on the lot within 10 minutes of their arrival.

This is to make you feel important, and to point you in the direction of the "hit cars". A lot of customers are sometimes caught off guard when a salesperson approaches this quickly. This is by design. **Salespeople are taught to get "control" of the customer quickly** and even the greeting is predesigned.

"Welcome to ABC motors, I'm Jackson and you are?"

This is designed to get your name quickly and effortlessly. They want your name quickly so they can use it over and over again during the initial greeting process. Why? Because they know your name is the sweetest sound to your ears, it also puts you at ease, and puts things in a relaxed and friendly environment. Everyone is now on a first name basis.

"So Bob, what can I get you a price on today?"

Again, another planned and strategic question that you can only answer by telling them what car you are interested in. Most times, the customer can say "we are just looking" or "we are not here to buy today".

The process has begun. From now on, everything that is said by the salesman is predesigned to put you on the **"road to the sale"**.

15.

Salesmen are trained to handle the "I'm just looking" customer, and also they hear customers say "I'm not buying today" probably 5 times a day.

It's actually funny because customers think they have given you a "smoke screen" but today's highly trained salesperson can quickly over come your objections. As I said earlier, today's salesperson is constantly trained to get control of you and the buying process. Just about every dealership in this country, trains its salespeople constantly on the "Road to a Sale".

Understanding the "Road to a Sale"

This is what they are taught in this numeric order. They don't go to the next step until they have completed the preceding step.

Meet and greet the customer.

Establish common ground.

Select a vehicle.

Present the vehicle.

Demonstrate the vehicle.

Inspect and drive the trade-in (with the customer).

Tour the dealership.

Write up and negotiate the deal.

Turn-over to Finance Department.

Deliver the vehicle.

Follow up the customer within three days of delivery.

These 11 steps are taught over and over, backwards and forwards, constantly drilled and re-drilled by dealerships every day. Salespeople even have a "mini" card that fits in their wallet or pocket with the "road to a sale" listed on it so it is available for immediate reference.

So now let's cover these 11 items because understanding the psychology behind each one **will better prepare you for the battle to come.**

Meet and Greet. As previously mentioned everything is planned and prepared for your visit. You have been strategically parked in a certain area, and a salesperson has greeted you with the aforementioned greeting. He knows your name and is trained to use it religiously.

Now he wants to make sure you're at ease and that everyone is there that is involved in making the decision to purchase. This way later in the negotiation process you can't say, "I need to run it by my wife or husband or whomever".

During this time **he may ask if the car you drove up in is going to be a trade-in.** He may even walk over to it and put his finger or hands on blemishes on your car. This is all predesigned to de-value your trade without even saying a word. He may touch the tires and the customer will offer up **"oh yeah, I was planning on replacing these tires".**

Establish common ground. This is when the salesperson will ask you questions that come in the form of casual conversation like "I see you have on a golf shirt, did you play today? Really? Where do you play Bob? I also play golf, that's a great course, very difficult, but a lot of fun, what do you usually shoot?

How long have you lived in the area? So Bob, are you from Florida? I was born and raised here…are you a Gator or a Seminole? Me too! **These are all just casual questions to put you at ease** and reinforce the use of your name. A smart professional salesperson will also get the wife involved as he knows women make up a huge percentage of the buying motive and decision.

Select a vehicle. This is where all the money is won or lost. What I mean by that is a professional salesperson understands that landing you on the right car the first time is paramount to both getting you to "fall in love" and making the most profit. Usually they come hand in hand. **The more you love the car, the more you will pay for it.**

Most salespersons will ask questions to make sure the right car is chosen. **"Not the right car for you, but the right car they can make the most money on"**. They also have to make sure they have qualified you enough to know what you can and can't afford, they are smart enough to know that if they show you, here is an example of some questions they may ask.

So Bob, I see you are driving a 4 door sedan, were you looking to stay in the same size or maybe smaller? Your car Bob, has cloth seats, is that ok or we're you looking to change that? What are some things about your current car that you would change if you could? How about the color?

Would your wife want to change that? Do you still owe money on your trade? What bank Bob is it financed with? How much are your payments each month?

Here is the result of those questions. The salesperson has an idea of what type of credit you have because he now knows what lender you have your car financed with. He knows the banks that only loan to people with great credit, and he knows the banks that specialize in bad credit.

He got your wife involved by asking her about color because he knows the female buyer is more of an emotional buyer and **is motivated by the five senses to make a selection, Feel, taste, smell, hear and see.**

While the man or husband is more logical in his dominate buying motive and would be more interested in technology related to items like engine size, gas mileage, warranty details etc. The salesperson now knows you were tired of the cloth seats in your old car and this time you want a car with all the bells and whistles, leather and navigation etc.

The salesperson is trained to make sure he doesn't show you a car that is too "loaded".

The reason is, because later on when he is negotiating with you, he wants to make sure he has you on the car that will fit your budget and also make the dealership the most money. If he shows you the top of the line model and you fall in love, which you will, he has a problem later if he **finds out the payments you want only works on a cheaper car.** A "rule of thumb" in the car business is **you can always go up in equipment, but you can rarely go down.**

After you've salivated on the loaded up car, you are not very likely to be ready to settle for the car with less features even if the payments are lower, because it's hard to settle for the model without leather after you have felt the plush soft palomino leather in the nice more expensive model.

He also knows you wanted the new back up camera that was not available when you bought your last car, and now has a good idea as to what car to show you.

Present and demonstrate the vehicle. This is one of the most practiced and rehearsed portions of their job. Not only are they routinely taught on the proper way to do a "walk around" presentation, but the factory sends out reps to do training and present on-line videos for them to become more proficient.

They are taught how to present the car from the moment they unlock it, to the moment you drive away on the demonstration ride. **Remember nothing happens by chance,** your will be given a facts and benefit presentation coupled with a **"trial close"** on every point that may sound something like this…

So Bob, this new ABC model comes with the latest greatest back up camera you asked about, this will enable you to see what is behind you when you back up and prevent you from backing into something, that is something you said you were interested in when you purchase your next vehicle isn't that right Bob? (Trial Close)

The "trial close" is simply an industry sales tactic designed to get an acknowledgement from you that you agree. You may nod your head or say "yes".

The salesperson is trained to get as many of those acknowledgements from you as he or she can during the product presentation, because that lets them know how they are doing because if you say "no" to something they can back up and address that objection.

It's basically a "temperature taker", just checking to see if you are saying "yes" and nodding your head, this tells the salesperson that so far he has you on the "right car".

The "trial close" is designed to get you to take mental ownership of the car and to envision yourself owning the car.

A good salesperson may try many of these "trial closes" along the way.

Mr. Customer, couldn't you see yourself parking this nice new car in the garage? Mr. Customer, wouldn't it be nice to take a long trip in your new car and not be worried about repairs?

Mr. Customer, isn't this model your absolute first choice? Mr. Customer, in which name will you be titling the car?

Mr. Customer did you bring your title to your trade in case we make a deal? Mr. Customer, you did say you wanted bluetooth in your new car? Hand me your phone and I will go ahead and "sync it" so you can hear your favorite songs on this amazing stereo system. And there are many more.

Watch for these the next time you are on a test drive. Marvel at the professional at work. Every time you agree to anything, a good salesperson knows you are one step closer to buying the vehicle.

After going through the car in a predetermined way, depending on the dealership, most salespeople are trained to end the presentation with you in the driver's seat with the engine running.

That is so they can easily get you to agree to test drive the vehicle. Some dealerships will ask for your driver's license and run in to make a copy and get a dealer tag to put on the vehicle.

They know that **their chances of selling you a car go up dramatically if you will test drive it.** A good salesperson understands that you wouldn't buy a car you have not driven.

A lot of dealerships won't allow the salesperson to present numbers to a customer that hasn't driven a car. Everything will stop and a manager or closer will come out and attempt to get you to drive the car before they work numbers.

Some customer's will simply stand at the side of the car where the window sticker is and start asking the salesperson about discounts and saying "I never pay sticker for any car I buy". "I'm not driving the car until you give me your best price!

I used to love these customers because they really are buyers. Here is what I would say. Mr. Customer, I appreciate the compliment, but I'm not that good. I'm not good enough to sell you a car on just price alone.

But, if you will give me a few minutes of your time to show you the features and benefits of the car, and best determine if this car fits your needs, then I will be glad to get you the best price. Because let's face it, if this car doesn't fit you wants or needs you won't buy it anyway! Is that fair?

Most customers would shrug and say, "Ok yeah, let's make sure this car has the equipment I need first."

There is nothing wrong with driving the car if you are serious about buying a car **I suggest you do drive it.** It's a huge investment. You need to make sure it has all the equipment you want and suits your needs for the next couple of years.

I'm just showing the psychology behind each step in the "road to a sale". You will be shown a predetermined route to drive the car typically a road without a lot of traffic where you can get up some speed and experience some tight turns to show off the cars handling abilities, followed up with a couple of trial closing questions along the way.

So Bob, how did the car feel in that turn back there? It was pretty amazing huh? What about the smooth acceleration? Isn't that something you could see yourself enjoying in your new vehicle? You nod yes.

After a series of many "yes's" the salesperson is feeling great, and will try to create excitement like putting the radio on your favorite station, or making sure the a/c is on to accentuate the new car smell, or demonstrating the lumbar seating for your back, all emotional hot buttons that will later play into the buying decision.

Upon returning to the dealership, he will instruct you to park in the new car in the "delivery" area because "Bob, **we don't want anyone to drive your new car while we are finalizing everything"**. This is deadly.

"90% of customers that agree to this statement buy a car."

A lot of customers won't disagree, but some will, by saying "well we need to see the numbers first and think on it a bit". Typically the final parking spot will be very close to your trade in.

Inspect and drive the trade in. This is gold. If the salesperson can pick apart your trade with you standing there, he stands to hold much more money later on the value of your car, which equals more profit for the dealer.

"I have had customers actually help me by telling me all the things that are wrong with the car, even though I didn't ask"

Remember, the salesperson understands that your car is like a member of your family, he is careful to not insult your car but will be subtle and precise by **gently place his hand or finger on dents, or scratches, or cracks in windshield or dash,** usually the customer will offer up "oh yeah that's when we backed into a shopping cart" or "yeah, little Johnny spilled grape juice on the seats".

I have had customers tell me later that they only agreed to the lower amount for the trade because they were embarrassed it wasn't clean or because of the imperfections that were pointed out. Conversely, **smart customers will have their trade- in professionally detailed and shined up.** This presents a problem for the salesperson and he understands that the customer came to "do battle".

During this process the salesperson may ask if you have the title or registration in your glove box. **This is also a trial close.** It tells the salesman you came to do business today, and that's what they want to hear. The last and most important "trial close" the salesperson can ask you before going into the dealership is...

"Bob, other than the numbers is there any reason why we can't wrap this up today?"

This is a crucial time in the buying experience. The answer you give to this question tells the salesperson the most important thing he needs to know **BEFORE** he takes you inside the dealership.

If you say no, then you are agreeing that you like the car, it is the car you would buy, you have no objections about the car, and now the only thing left to discuss are the numbers.

That's all a good salesperson can ask for. **He has done his job.** Now, if you don't buy the car for whatever reasons like the payments are too high, or your credit, or whatever, he has done his job. He landed you on the car you wanted that should fit in your budget, and he got you to say you would buy the car if the number or figures were agreeable. He is not worried about the rest of the process. He knows he has trained and highly motivated managers/closers to help "push you over the edge".

Tour of the dealership. This is just a continuation of the "dog and pony show" that has been going on so far, the salesperson will walk you over to the service manager and the parts manager and anyone else that will listen and say you are a new customer purchasing a new ABC model and here is where you will come to schedule your first service appointment.

Again a huge trial close and moving the sale further down the road to success. They may offer you a beverage, show your kids where the playroom is and get them logged on or playing video games.

Then introduce you to the sales manager who will be doing all the numbers, the salesperson will show you his scrap book of previous customers, show you awards the dealership has won etc…then place you at his desk or work station. On his desk usually are strategically, placed pictures of his children and family to again, build some common ground and personalize his or her self.

Write up and negotiating the deal. This is the culmination of everything that has gone on so far. Hopefully by now the salesperson has "bonded" with you and your family, found common ground, shown you pictures of his family on his desk to "humanize" himself, and it's time to begin the process to discuss numbers.

Every dealership has its own form or document that the salesperson uses to start the flow of information. **Today, all dealerships use a CRM computer sales management tool.**

Gone are the days of doing everything by hand and on paper. The salesperson will take your current address off your title or registration, and remember, he made a copy of your license before the test drive, and loads it into the computer on his desk which then will populate to the sales managers computer at the sales "tower" which is the hub where the managers sit. Salespersons are not allowed behind the sales tower desk and from here the entire deal is worked.

This is where the salesperson goes to present your offer or discuss the deal. Once the deal is properly loaded in the CRM the salesperson will pull out a printed worksheet with all of your name, address, phone number etc…your trade information, any payoff information, your lender and **then try to culminate all the previous trial closes into the main one now"** Bob, as you know we have spent some time together, and I believe we have found the perfect car for your needs and desires.

You've indicated that "if we get all the numbers worked out you would own the car today". **Would you initial that here?** There usually is a statement hard printed on dealership worksheets at the bottom that says **"Customer will buy today if terms are agreeable"**

He takes that work sheet to the sales desk where managers are, along with a set of the keys to your trade and gives all of it to the desk to wait for figures. The "desk" will send out the used car manager to appraise your trade, come up with a value and then the sales manager will send the salesperson back to present the numbers to you.

Now a comment about initialing in the space provided saying you will buy today if terms are agreeable. This is the ultimate "trial close" since you are starting to sign paperwork giving your approval.

The manager will use this initialing later against you if you don't buy the car. He will say "Mr. Customer you signed right here saying you would buy the car, are you not a man of your word? This puts most customers on their heels.

The manager is playing on your "good word" to make sure you buy the car. We are going to discuss strategies later so for now let's assume the numbers get worked out and a deal is made.

Turnover to Finance & Insurance Office. This stands for the Finance and Insurance department. Once the numbers are agreed up the desk "pushes" the deal via the computer to the next available finance manager which works on straight commission, (We will discuss pay plans later) on the products they sell and its first come first serve. Simply meaning the next available finance manager gets the next available customer.

Usually while you are filling out the necessary documents with the salesperson the finance manager will come out and introduce him or herself to you and say "nice to meet you", congratulations Mr. Customer, I will be finalizing your paperwork and I should only be a few minutes and I will come back to get you.

He goes back in his office begins to print all his forms, and gets his menu presentation ready to sell you his extra products and services. We will go into more detail later on the strategies to avoid the finance manager's huge profit product presentation.

Deliver the vehicle. After you have completed your time with finance, he will page your salesperson to come get you, and he will then take you to the service manager to schedule your first appointment.

The car would have already been detailed and cleaned, and should be waiting in the delivery area, where he goes over all the features of the car, your books and manuals, replaces your tag, asks for a good survey, and says goodbye.

Follow up with the customer. This is when the salesperson calls you within 3 days of delivery to ensure everything is going well with your vehicle, ask for referrals, and remind you of the factory survey that will be emailed to you and to please give him all "10s" for every question, as it effects his status with the dealership and him only.

(Which is not true, it effects the entire dealership) more on factory surveys later.

Congratulations! You have seen the entire planned and rehearsed chain of events regarding what happens when you pull up to a dealership, hopefully understanding that nothing is left to chance.

Chapter 3

How Dealership Employees Get Paid
Including the Dealer

The Basic Salesperson Pay Plan. Don't be fooled by today's high tech world and "no haggle" car buying experiences or even dealerships that say they don't work off commission anymore...don't believe it.

The salesman will even say they are there to "work for you" and will play the role of mediator between you and the sales manager. They will say, **"My job is to make sure you get the best price today"**

And that's partly true, the best price is **the price that you agree to, and that they make the most commission off of**. Most salespersons today work off what is called a "draw system". Basically how it works is they are paid minimum wage for the hours they work for the month.

However, at the end of the month, they receive a commission check for all the deals and commission earned from those deals during the month. Then the money already paid to them "the draw" for the hours they worked is subtracted from the monthly commission check.

"There are two profit sides to every car deal".

There is the front side of the deal and the back end of the deal. The front is the sale of the car including price, trade allowance etc. Then there is the back end of the deal where the dealership makes money on the financing portion of the transaction.

"Typically most dealerships pay a salesperson one way and one way only, ON THE PROFIT"

So here's how it works, the dealership has a hard cost they pay for every car. The amount of money made over their true cost is the profit or "gross" on the deal. The salesperson will get approximately 30% of the gross profit from the sale of the car.

<u>**Most dealerships average $1250 to $1800 profit on the front**</u> sale of the car so the salesperson would make around $450.

Then when the customer goes into the business office, they will purchase and extended warranty, gap insurance, wheel and tire protection, theft protection, GPS tracking systems, interior and paint protection not to mention the profit the dealership made on the interest rate mark up or "reserve profit".

Even though the salesperson had little to do with this portion of the sales process, most dealerships pay them around 3% of the finance profit and since most finance departments average around $1400 profit on each car sold that's an additional $45 to the salesperson.

Also, the dealership pays bonuses for numbers of units sold, typically they would receive $1000 for 15 cars sold, and **even if the dealership sells a car and LOSES money,** the salesperson is paid a minimum or "mini" commission of around $100. But it doesn't stop there.

The manufacturer or factory also pay the salesperson around $100 up to $500 for each new car sold which is loaded onto a debit card that is mailed to them. So all in all, there are salespeople that are really good at what they do making serious money. I have worked with many salespeople that routinely make 6 figures.

Remember, **they only make the real money when they make serious profit on the car deal.** Salespeople that routinely sell cars for "minis" don't last.

The hours are too long and the job is too demanding. I'm not advocating that there is anything wrong with them making a nice living.

However, my purpose in writing this book is to **help you buy a car at the lowest possible profit to the dealer.** Believe me they make plenty of profit on the cars they sell. Just don't let them make it all up on you.

The Sales Managers Pay Plan. Today's sales managers are paid some serious money. They work long hours and have to manage and train the salespeople that work for them. They have to manage the inventory and make sure they hit all the sales objectives set by the factory for their dealership.

How are they paid? Just like the salespeople, **on the profit that is generated from each sale.** If all the deals for the month are "minis" they make nothing and probably get fired. It doesn't matter how many cars a month they sell, they are not paid on volume, but profit!

They also get paid on the front and the back of a car deals profits. **A hidden inside profit center is a large amount of money that is earned by the dealership each month if they meet or exceed the factory quota in sales and customer satisfaction.** Typically, a new car dealer will earn $500 per car for each new car sold at the end of the months.

Also if their customers return excellent customer satisfaction index scores or CSI, they receive even more money that goes into a pot that all the managers and the Dealer get paid on.

Without reading this book, chances are you would never have known about this hidden profit. It's not publicized. The factory or the dealers never mention this money in their advertising. It's pure profit only to them and it's a huge part of whether or not they will have a good month.

So when the month is over, and all the profits are added up, the managers get around 3% to 4% of the total gross profit.

"I have run dealerships that have generated a million dollars a month in gross profits"

I have worked with sales managers that make upwards to $250,000 per year. **The reason I am telling you this is so you can realize that everything evolves, around profit.**

As I said, making a profit if not a dirty word, however, the **purpose of this book is to not let them make it all off you.**

Finance Managers Pay Plans. Finance managers only get paid on the products that they sell you AFTER you have agreed to buy the car.

They offer to finalize the paperwork and process your tag and title work, all the while they are only placed in that office to produce PROFIT. Everything they offer to sell you has enormous markup.

As I said a good Finance Manager will average $1400 profit on every car sold. They get upwards to 20% of the profit they generate, most good ones make around

$170,000 per year plus they receive bonuses from the company that represents the extended warranties they sell.

General Managers Pay Plans. The General Manager oversees the entire dealership, not only sales but service and parts, again also massive profit centers. They receive a percentage of the total NET profit of the dealership once the month is complete. That means after all expenses and salaries are paid, whatever profit remains, they receive a percentage of. The last dealership I was General Manager of generated an income to me of around $400,000. You may be asking yourself why I would leave a career that generated that much income and write this book. Great question....I came to the realization that I possessed this knowledge and after looking around realized nobody was sharing it!

"I wanted to educate and empower consumers on the second largest purchase of their lives.

How the Dealer Get's Paid. Obviously the Dealer is the guy at the end of the line. He owns the franchise which is the name of the dealership. He owns the property that the dealership sits on. He owns the buildings that the dealerships operate out of.

He also owns the warranty company that sells the extended warranties in the finance office. He also owns the "blue sky", that is a term used in the car business to represent all the future business his dealership will do with its present and future customer base.

There is huge monetary value placed on the "blue sky" when negotiating the sale or purchase of a dealership. Most dealers are not involved in the day to day operations of the dealership, he doesn't meet with customers or handle complaints, he has managers that do that.

He is the man behind the scenes rarely can you find the dealer at the dealership. He is completely insulated by a line of employees and normally considered "absentee". But make no mistake about it he is the man in charge. The GM runs the business and answers to the dealer.

"Most successful dealers are multi-millionaires".

"I last worked for a dealer that made $700,000 Profit in one month!"

Why am I telling you this? Or why do you need to know?

"Because you need to prepare yourself for battle"

You have no idea of the planning and plotting that is taking place to prepare for your arrival and I dare say….**the average consumer is ill prepared for the task at hand**. So if you are planning on buying a new car at a new car dealership and by reading this book you save thousands of dollars, then I did my job. **I have made millions of dollars selling cars.** It's time to educate and assist today's consumer with up to date relevant inside information on how to negotiate and successfully purchase your dream car without paying too much!

Chapter 4

Getting Ready for Battle.

So which buyer are you? There are many types out there but for the sake of time let's narrow it down to the ones that are most prevalent in today's market. **Salespeople are trained to search out what type of buyer you are and form a strategy to overcome any objections you may have.**

In order to combat these strategies from the dealer you must understand your dominant buying motive or "DBM".

The Logical Buyer. The logical buyer is the one that uses the logistical portion of the brain to make purchasing decisions. He does all the research, he studies reviews, reads all the latest car magazines, understands things like gear ratios, turning radius, horsepower, slip differential, torch, drag, gas mileage and subscribes to all the buyer websites(more on these later).

He typically knows more about the car than the salesperson selling it. He isn't easily convinced just because he is told something is true. He wants to know how things work and why they work, he has plenty of time on his hands to make an informed decision.

He won't be rushed or tricked by time restraints or special offers that only last for short period of time. **In the car business world, this customer is the least liked.** Simply because you never know how you stand with him. He won't tell you if he likes the car, or anything about the car, he gives the impression he could "take it or leave it".

As a salesperson you can't "take his temperature" by using trial closes. He shows no affinity to things like color, or gimmicks on cars, he simply will buy only when he has done all his due diligence and when he comes on the lot, he is coming for a specific car.

He won't be talked into a "switch car" or a low advertised price car. He knows exactly what he wants. He probably visited his credit union and had them check his credit to find out what his score is and also found out what interest rate they would offer him.

He's studied up on extended warranties and gap insurance and whether it's something that has real value. Most of these customers tend to be engineers, mechanical people, teachers, blue collar technical employees, retired military or active duty military. They can also be defined by ethnicity. Buyers from countries like India or Russia, are slow to make decisions and hard to sell. Most salespeople hate to deal with these customers. They will run inside and grab a manager for a quick "T.O" or turnover.

"Please come talk to my customer, I can't land him on a car, he won't come in the building, I'm losing him...you better come quick"! These customers do buy cars. But they don't fit into the dealership mentality that "only lives for today".

"Dealerships believe there is no tomorrow".

If they don't sell you a car today, they will never see you again. And I must say it's mostly true. Studies show that the chances a customer will return to the dealership and choose to purchase are less than 10%.

That's why they try so hard to get you to "buy today"! They will go to any means to ensure you come back. One tried and true method to guarantee you return is to talk you into taking the new car home overnight. It's called "de-horsing".

That's when you leave your trade-in and drive the new car home to "think about it" or show the other decision maker like the wife or significant other. **They have to come back now for sure because they are in the car!**

<u>The Emotional Buyer.</u> **This is a car salespersons dream.** They are everything that he Logical buyer is not. They will often say "I didn't even come here to buy a car today"!

43.

They will respond to ridiculous advertisements like the direct mail piece mailer we discussed that says "you won 25,000 dollars come claim your prize" or "come get your gold coins" **and they end up buying a car.**

They are completely unprepared, have no idea what their current car is worth, really don't have specifics on what car they want, a lot of times they don't know what their current credit situation is (another dream customer) and are easily influenced by their emotions.

A good salesperson recognizing this will point out features on the car that respond to the 5 senses we previously mentioned. "Look at the glossy paint", "feel this imported leather", "smell this new car aroma", "isn't it quiet when it runs", and "how about this luxurious ride" isn't it amazing!

All the while the customer is completely wrapped up in the emotion or "high of the experience" which takes their attention off what is really important like the numbers or their budget etc.

They look at their old dirty trade next to the shiny new car and their done. I've actually have had these customer's say "can I go ahead and start switching my things into the new car?"

"BEFORE WE WORKED ANY NUMBERS"!

This is the ultimate "impulse buyer" and salespeople love it. These are the ones that generate everyone's paycheck.

Not only do they love the car, but they love the salesperson, the deal, promise to send in a perfect factory survey, and the dealership made $5000 off them!

Unfortunately, these buyers tend to go home and the "ether wears off" or they get buyer's remorse and come back the next day to unwind the entire transaction.

As I am writing this book in the state of Florida, there is a clause on Florida dealer retail installment contracts that is binding and legal that has a huge block close to the bottom that says in bold print, **"There is no cooling off period on this purchase, you can't simply change your mind and return the car"** I can't tell you how many people

I have had to show that contract to along with their signature at the bottom. Again, **if you are this type of buyer, this book is for you.**

The Credit Customer. Another favorite of the dealership world is the credit customer. This customer comes in two catagories. They either have poor credit and just want a car, also known as a "get me done" or they THINK they have poor credit when actually they have good credit but

45.

are never told, **so the finance manager can make more money by overcharging them on the interest rate.**

Also, these customers are sometimes told they must purchase additional products offered by the finance manager because the bank said to do so.

As soon as a trained salesperson whiffs out that this customer has credit issues, **they stop what they are doing and run the customer inside to check their credit** and the manager tells the salesperson what car to show them. He knows what the bank will approve for this customer and picks the car the dealership can make the most profit on. It is not the car the customer necessarily wants.

They tell the customer to make their payments on time on this car, and then later they can come back and trade the car in and step up to a nicer car. This customer typically can come from many walks of life. **They are just uninformed.**

The dealership takes the opportunity to ensure the most money is made on these customers and it makes up for the ones that came in "educated" and they didn't make any money off them.

A lot of the time, dealerships have a dedicated department solely working to get people with poor credit approved. I know of a dealership that won't let salespeople show anyone a car until they first bring the customer inside and "check their credit".

These people will end up with lenders that charge the dealer a huge "bank fee" as much as $4000 dollars just to finance the deal. The dealer simply passes that fee on to the customer or takes it out of his profit.

It's an ugly business, many times the bank repossesses the car because the customer can't or won't make the payments, or was pushed into a payment they can't afford. In Florida the maximum interest rate, that can be charged on a new car is 16.49% and on a used car it's 24.99%, see what that does to your payments!

The Buried Buyer. This customer is the one that trades cars so quickly he never gets time to gain or catch up on his cars value to what his payoff is. Simply put he is "upside down". He owes a lot more than the car is worth.

The other reason he is so buried is the last dealer made $6000 profit off his deal and that profit was added to his loan. So now, instead of owing $15,000 on his $15,000 car, he owes $21,000 on his $15,000 car and he is $6000 upside down.

The problem with this is two things, the salesperson has to tell him how buried he is so now he knows they blasted him and will never return, or the banks won't approve the customer on another purchase because they won't loan more money than what a vehicle typically is worth.

For example, say Mr. Customer wants to trade in his car and buy a new one. He has $6000 negative equity on his trade. This has to be rolled onto the loan for the new car and it has another $6000 in profit and taxes and fees so now the bank is asked to loan $12,000 more than the new car is worth.

The problem is if the bank has to repossess the car and take it to auction, they stand to lose a minimum of $12,000! **In my experience 8 out of 10 customers have negative equity.** It's a common thing, **cars are simply not appreciating assets** like a house they will drop in value as much as 35% when you drive off the lot.

Even though you only just bought the car and drove it home like 10 miles, the car is now considered "used", not new anymore and the book has a lesser value for that car now.

There are ways to avoid negative equity like having a large down payment, or trade equity, or **NOT OVER PAYING FOR YOUR NEXT PURCHASE!**

I want to give you an illustration of a deal I did myself not all too long ago. Late one Saturday afternoon, an elderly man came in to drive one of our new convertibles. It had to be a convertible. Well, the manufacturer I worked for only had 2 different models.

He knew about the first car, but after the test drive, he showed no interest so I suggested the "other convertible" model which was a car he had never considered. He agreed to drive the car and it worked. He liked the car. He had a fairly new Lexus sedan that was paid off, he didn't owe any money on the car.

Long story short I held $10,000 or "under allowed" on its true value by $10,000 and charged him full "addendum" not sticker, for my new car. (We will cover the addendum sticker later). **The front end of the deal was like $14,000....**the next day here he came back after the "ether wore off" and didn't want the car.

I showed him the contract he had signed and told him I could not undo the deal. Obviously, he was upset. He went next door to our sister dealership and traded in the new car he just bought from us to them.

They didn't know our products so they called me for a figure on what his car was worth. This car was almost $45,000 the day before and he had put like 50 miles on it. I offered to buy the car from the dealership if they took it in on trade for $38,000.

They made the deal and I bought back the car and sold it a week later for $42,000! That one deal generated over $20,000 in profit to the dealer.

 Now that does not happen very often but it does illustrate a term often used in the car business "switch and get rich" simply put, **find a emotional buyer and switch them to the car you want to sell them and here comes the profit.**

The strategy I am going to teach you involves a little of each one of these buyers. You will have a proven strategy and ensure the story I just illustrated never happens to you.

Chapter 5

Buying the New Car.

Okay, so we've educated you on how the basic dealership structure works, how everyone is paid, how the advertising works and hopefully you have identified what type of buyer you are so we can talk about strategy, the reason you bought this book right!

Ok, so step one is, **you must know true cost**. Before you even set foot on a dealerships property you must have an idea of what true cost of the car is, and how many rebates and incentives are on the car you are trying to buy.

For this chapter, don't worry about your trade in, or the financing, or anything else, you need to focus and do some homework to be prepared to know what true cost is on the new car. First off, let me say **a dealer will lose money on a car and they do it every day.**

You may be sitting there asking yourself well if I knew true cost on the car I wanted I wouldn't need this book.

Not true. Here's why. In my 25 years in the car business the industry itself has changed a lot. Due to the availability of the internet there is a plethora of information readily available to anyone that dare look. Problem is nobody does.

I can honestly say that in the last 5 years of running dealerships I have on maybe 2 occasions had customers come in with a number that was close to true cost on our car. How can this be you ask? With all the data that is around? Are people not looking? No.

They are. **They are just uninformed**. Here is what I mean. One popular method you can subscribe to is a service free service called TrueCar.com. Its commercials are all over the television advertising how you can get the "no haggle" true car price and simply print off the certificate with the price listed for the car you want and take it into the dealership and get your deal. Wow, **wish it was that easy.**

But here is how true car works. You log in an open a free account. Then once you have put in your zip code and model of car you are looking for, say a 2015 Nissan Altima S, it will show you the three closest Nissan dealerships to your zip code, and the prices of the car from each one. One will be lowest of the three by a couple hundred dollars. You show up at the dealership present the certificate and pick up your car.

The dealer is the one that pays TrueCar, $299 for a new car. TrueCar searches the dealer's registrations against their own records to find a match, then they send the dealer a bill for that deal and if the dealer doesn't pay, they are cut off from being offered by TrueCar.

Now in today's competitive new car market, what dealer doesn't want or need a new car deal? **The factory reps are always putting pressure on dealers to take and sell more new cars.**

If the dealer falls too far below required monthly expectations, the factory can come in and remove the franchise, or give it to another dealer that wants it and has a proven track record. Remember that "blue sky" we talked about earlier, big bucks if a dealer loses his franchise. But back to TrueCar.

What the **customer does not know** is that the dealer is ready for the deal.

When you come in with that certificate, **how do you know it's the dealers true cost?** You don't, you only know it's the cheapest price of the 3 closest dealers.

So based on our example of a Nissan Altima, let's say the lowest price in your area is $18,995 plus tax, tag, title, and dealer fees. Now when you show up with the certificate the salesperson will say "absolutely no problem" and here is the car.

You go on the test drive as usual and all is well. However, when you get to the negotiations on price and present the certificate, the salesperson takes it up to the manager, and comes back with the following questions; are you active military?

Are you a college graduate having graduated in the last two years? Are you a previous Nissan lease customer coming out of a lease and leasing another car? Are you going to finance with Nissan Motor Acceptance?

Why all the questions? Because each one of these questions represents **a rebate or customer cash amount that is used to get to the true car price** and the price of $18,999 represents that you qualify for all these incentives.

"So in order to get the cheapest price, you must qualify for every single rebate or incentive that the factory happens to be offering that month".

And nobody ever does. So the manager will say well Mr. Customer, you don't qualify for this one that's an extra $500 I must add to the price, and you don't qualify for that one that's an extra $1000 that must be added and oh, you're not financing with NMAC?

You wanted to pay cash? That's another $500 we must add back so now what is the price?

Let's see. $18,999 plus $2000 in non qualifying rebates and incentives equals $20,999 plus tax, tag and title, and dealer fees. That's your price for the car, let's get this all wrapped up for you!

Meanwhile even though your head is spinning, you see the logic in what they did, and the car is the one you wanted with the right color and all, (emotional buyer) and your tired from work, why not go ahead a head and do it. Boom! What did the dealer make?

Let's assume you had no trade, great credit, and were paying cash.

"The dealer made a profit in 4 areas".

He made approximately $950 off the sale of the car, he got another $600 in hidden factory money called "hold back" this is hidden on the invoice. The factory pays the dealer on each car which averages about 3% of the invoice to offset advertising, transportation etc…and you also paid the $699 dealer fee which is pure profit, and the dealer had another $500 in hidden "dealer cash".

Dealer cash is similar to a rebate except the dealer does not have to give the dealer cash to the customer, the rebates he does, if you qualify.

Customers rarely know that it even exists. The dealer can keep the dealer cash and show it as profit on the deal, or pass the money along to the customer to make the deal happen. Dealer cash on a new car can be anywhere from $500 to a $1000.

"You can get the dealer to give you his dealer cash, you just have to know how ask for it."

So what's the damage? Looks like the dealer made $2749 minus the fee he has to pay to TrueCar of $299 which nets him a profit of $2450. Any dealer would take that on a new car deal every day.

But you're asking how did this just happen? "I thought these internet car buying sites were supposed to save me money? How is this saving me money? It isn't.

Because using the internet to get the best price is not how to get the best price. How about Edmunds.com, can't I go there and get the invoice price on any car I want?

Yes you can, but again, does it represent true dealer cost as the dealer knows it. <u>**What the internet can never show you is what the dealer actually shows as the true cost of the car.**</u>

If you had not read this book, you would not know about all the hidden money the dealer has at his disposal such as, holdback and dealer cash, and the factory incentive money for hitting his objectives. No website car buying service will tell you this. So what can you do? You won't believe how simple this is....

"You ask the dealer for the invoice at the dealership"

That's right you pick out the car you want, let the salesperson work all the numbers and simply ask to see the invoice on the car. **If they won't show it to you, get up and leave,** don't worry someone else will.

Trust me when I say I have worked thousands of car deals. I have seen every type of customer and heard every objection. The one thing that stops managers in their tracks is when a customer wants to see the invoice.

Most managers today, figured you saw it on the internet anyway so what the" heck". Also, back on the lot while you were looking at the window sticker did you happen to notice the **additional sticker** that is long and slender with added items like paint protection and mud flaps and pinstripes and wheel locks?

Did you also notice the extra price that was added for all these items? **This is called the "bump sticker".** Once the car gets to the lot from the factory, there is only one sticker on the car with the true "manufactures suggested retail price" or MSRP.

That came from the factory. But **once the dealer got the car he added the additional "bump sticker price"** that often can add up to $3000 over and above the MSRP!

When the numbers are presented at the salespersons desk, the first number they are trained to show is the "bump sticker price" or addendum price. They can't call it the MSRP because it's not. So they invented another term to explain the extra price they are now charging which is over and above the MSRP price and it's called the "list price". Not the MSRP!

Most customers don't catch the "bump" and will allow the dealership to work off this top number, not recognizing that this money is Pure Profit!

When you are looking at a new car on the lot, look where the original sticker is that came from the factory. It will be large and have all the equipment that comes on the car, all the options that are on the car, and which dealer the car was sent to originally, what port the car came to when it entered the country and so on.

"You can't miss it. It's put on the window at the factory".

Now look beside that sticker. Do you see a long thinner sticker that does not have the detail information the other bigger sticker has? It will have the dealer's logo and the car's stock number. That is simply a number the dealer assigned the car so that they can track the car. The factory never assigns a stock number to a car.

You will also see the make and model, and then it will have several items that have been added to the car AFTER it arrived at the dealership. In other words, dealers know that the difference between the MSRP price suggested by the factory and the price they paid for the car does not contain a lot of "markup profit".

This amount has diminished over the years. Some Korean import manufacturers only leave the dealer around $400 in profit even if they sell the car for MSRP.

So years back dealers found a way to charge more than the factory sticker by adding superfluous items to the car and making huge profits off them, all those things added only cost the dealer about $250 in cost, and they charged you $2950! Always be aware of this extra sticker and on the lot, tell the salesperson **you don't want these items that were added or you simply don't want to pay for them.**

The salesperson is trained to say Mr. Customer, we already added these items to the car they can't be taken off and all of our cars come with these items on them, (they don't and chances are you can find one on the back of the lot that has not had the extra's put on yet).

These cars won't have an addendum sticker added yet. It should only get added when the items are put on the car in the service department. I have had instances when the car on the lot did have an "addendum or bump sticker" and the extra items were never put on the car.

"Never allow the dealer to work from the "bump sticker" it's pure dealer profit."

You may be saying to yourself I've heard to ask for the invoice before, well nobody does, and it's a killer to the dealer. There is simply no way to overcome a customer asking to see the invoice.

"The beauty of this strategy is you are now working from cost up, not profit down."

Truth is, the dealer will and should produce the invoice and here is why. As we previously discussed, all new car dealers have a monthly and quarterly sales quota based on their location set by the factory.

The smart guys that make the cars, have these market analyst that do all this research and look at how many registrations are taking place in your town, and how many cars this particular dealer sold last year, and they come up with what is called the "dealers retro number".

This means the dealer must sell say 125 new cars that month AND reach an acceptable satisfaction survey level from the new car customers that they sold. If they do sell 125 cars and have excellent CSI, they are at 100% of their factory objective, and this typically earns them an additional $500 plus for each car they sold that month all the way back to the first one sold.

So some easy math means the **dealer earned around $65,000 additional profit for the month from the factory. You the customer NEVER see this money.**

60.

Now the beauty of this "retro" money is they don't have to pay the salespeople commission on it, only the managers get paid on it. And the manager's control what deals are taken and what deals are passed on based on how close they are to hitting their number that month.

So as a manager you have to ask yourself, if I get a huge bonus when we hit this retro money, **why do I care if we lose money on some deals here and there?** They understand that to hit the number set by the factory they have to take the good with the bad, meaning they need huge profit deals to offset the loser deals that will come.

Now factor in that it's getting close to the end of the month and the dealership is not tracking or "pacing" enough new car sales to hit their retro and in walks you and you are offering to purchase a new car, you just want to see the invoice. That is why everyone knows that …

"The best time to buy a new car, is towards the end of the month, hands down"

If the dealer needs 25 more new cars and there are only 3 days left in the month, they will take pretty much any offer proposed on a new car. I've seen dealers lose up to $4000 on a new car deal when they are trying to hit the retro.

Why would they not? What's a $4000 loser when they stand to collect $65,000 in retro money from the factory? Another important thing to mention is the pressure the managers are under that comes from not earning the monthly retro money. First, and most importantly the **Dealer himself is upset that he didn't get that money.**

Second, the factory is not happy the dealership failed to hit their monthly objectives because they forecasted to their board of directors how many new cars they would sell during this month and they are going to come in below what was projected.

And third, all the managers missed out on the additional income from the lost retro money. **Managers get fired when they miss the retro.**

Dealerships get put on "notice" that the store is underperforming by the factory. Meetings are scheduled, the Dealer has to show up and that's not good. Heads will roll. The factory retro money and **hitting the monthly sales objective set by the factory is mandatory** in today's new car dealership world.

"All new car manufacturer's whether domestic or import, use the "retro system" to motivate dealers to sell more new cars".

Recently, I encountered a customer that completely changed my mind set on how to sell cars. Even though I had been in the business for over 25 years, and felt as if I had heard every single objection there was to not buy a car, a man in his mid 50's strolled in and changed everything.

He let the salesperson do his "thing" and demonstrate the car. He even agreed to come in and give out some information to fill out the worksheet. But here is what happened next; he abruptly asked the salesperson to" **go get the manager"**.

This never happens most customers are scared to death of the managers or closers and will do anything to avoid them.

They don't have any rapport with the manager, have never met him, and have spent all their time with the salesperson that did build rapport and common ground.

But needless to say I was summoned. I came over introduced myself to the customer and this is what he said. "Look, I understand that you need to make money off these cars, I know how this works, I'm not stupid enough to believe you can operate this enormous facility, pay all these people, and not make a profit, however in this case, you won't.

"Here is my offer. I will buy this new car right now, but you're not going to make any money off me. This is my offer, take it or leave it. Now, please bring me your invoice on the car, and I will pay you exactly what you paid for the car.".

"This will be painless, and if you treat me right, I will tell my friends, fill out a great survey which you need, and you will get another new car deal that according to my calculations based on the time of the month, you desperately need. Wow, I was speechless for the first time in my career".

This guy just presented the perfect way to buy a new car. He asked for the invoice, he understood I needed several new car deals to hit my number, and he asked for the invoice!

So, I went and printed out the invoice, brought it over to the customer and he looked it over. Then he asked about the dealer "holdback" amount. Remember that? We talked about it earlier in the book.

"Dealer holdback is the hidden money that the factory pays to the dealer for each new car sold"

It is typically around 3% of the invoice price so, on a $20,000 car the dealer would receive around $600. **This money is completely hidden in the dealership,** only the managers, accounting and the dealer know about this money. The salespeople don't get paid on it, only the managers and the dealer.

The mistake most customers make when they ask for the invoice is they don't know about the holdback amount.

It's sometimes hidden on the invoice in code, or for most import manufacturers not on the invoice at all.

You have to ask what the amount is, and the manager will be so surprised you even know about it, he will usually tell you what it is. But just in case he doesn't, you know how to do the math.

Let's cover a misconception about dealer invoices. Many customers will say, how do I know that is the real invoice? Think about that. You think managers get so many requests to see the invoice that they keep a book with fake ones, just to fool the customer?

Trust me when I say, that does not happen because it never comes up. They don't have fakes or invoices with inflated numbers on them. That would take up way too much time.

But, let's go back to my customer. He then asked "how much the holdback was on this car"? I was shocked he knew what that was but I told him. Then he did the next best thing. **He asked me "how much the rebates and incentives from the factory were" on this particular model.** (We will cover rebates and incentives later).

I told him. He did some quick math, took the invoice amount reduced it by the holdback and rebates available.

Then he asked if there was any dealer cash on the vehicle, again I was surprised he knew what that was, and finally offered to buy the car for total amount (invoice minus holdback, rebates/incentives and dealer cash) and he was **not going to pay the dealer fee which he knew was pure profit.**

I was amazed, **I had never seen a customer work a deal that way.** It was perfection. Obviously, I took the deal, the customer bought the car and rolled away happy.

So let's review, the steps to successfully buy a new car and not pay profit.

Never pay the "bump" or addendum sticker added by the dealer. It's pure profit.

Ask to see the dealer invoice.

Ask how much the dealer hidden "holdback amount" is, or calculate it yourself. (3% of the cars invoice amount should be close)\

Ask about all the rebates and incentives and dealer cash available.

Subtract the holdback and rebates and dealer cash from the invoice amount. Get your final price.

Never pay the dealer fee, it gets added to the sales price later so you have to be careful it doesn't get slipped in.

Congratulations! **You just beat the dealer at his own game.** Depending on what time of the month you are trying to buy the car, no dealer will refuse to sell you a car at zero profit. Now keep in mind that a smart manager should take a new car deal ANY TIME he can, no matter what time of the month it is.

So remember, they need new car deals, and you are offering to help them hit their "retro number".

Now what about the salesperson? Don't feel sorry for him. As I mentioned before, he will get a minimum commission around $100 plus his factory money loaded onto his debit card and another $100 and be one deal closer to the dealership bonus money.

It truly is a "win-win" situation all around, you got the deal you wanted, the dealer got a new car deal, and the salesperson made a couple of bucks just for filling out the paperwork. Sometimes the dealer will try to switch you to another car that is older (since he is losing money) but usually it has the same equipment and color so if it's ok with you say that's fine.

Why does the dealer want to switch you to an older car? Well remember when I said that the factory gets paid by the dealer even before the car arrives on the lot? Well the Dealer doesn't use his own money to buy that car. He uses an outside bank.

This bank actually owns all the new cars and some of the used cars on the lot. They charge the dealer a fee for this, it's called "floor-planning". Every day that car sits on the lot, interest is being charged on that car. I've seen new cars sit on the lot for 6 to 8 months. Every day they sit they pile up floor-plan interest.

So the dealer has serious incentive to sell that car, especially when you come in and they are not making any money anyway. **Many times you can ask the dealer if they have another car just like the one you want only older. This is the car to get the best deal on.**

Understanding what motivates a dealer and how he gets his money will help you know what buttons to push to get the best deal. **I promise you, no one knows this information outside the dealership world.**

"You can even offer to pay UNDER invoice on this car, and the dealer will do it depending on its age!"

Offer to buy the oldest version available of the car you want on the lot. Depending on the manufacturer you can see when the car was delivered to the dealership by looking at the bottom corner of the factory sticker it will show a date the car was delivered.

Another great strategy is to offer to buy last year's model that the dealer still has not sold. You can wait until the next model year vehicles arrive on the lot then buy the car that is still new but from last year. So basically you could buy a 2014 model even though the 2015 model has hit the ground.

Dealers are eager to sell the remaining previous year models. There are advantages and disadvantages to this strategy.

The advantages are the older 2014 model will have more rebates and incentives and dealer cash than the 2015. Depending on how long the 2015 model has been available, it may have NO rebates or incentives yet.

So the 2014 model will be a lot cheaper. This can translate to getting a car with more features and options that would normally be out of your price range on a 2015.

Also the factory has been putting pressure on the dealers to get rid of old 2014 inventory. They are constantly reminded the dealers how they rank in their sales district against over dealers. The dealer never wants to be the guy at the bottom of that list with the most cars from last year.

The disadvantages to buying an older model car can be the cars left over do not have popular colors or options. That is why they didn't sell in the first place. For instance, in Florida if the dealer is stupid enough to order "all wheel drive" SUVs, they will usually sit forever because there isn't much use for these vehicles in Florida where it never snows.

The main disadvantage is the older car has already accumulated a year's worth of depreciation. If in say 3 years you want to trade the car in, it will be appraised as a 4 year old car. That effect's the value. But if you are the rare customer that plans on keeping the car for a long time, this could be an option for you.

Most manufacturers don't change body styles on cars very often, so chances are the both year models will look the same, or have the same body style. Your neighbor won't know what year you purchased.

Again, you must know what motivates the dealer to give away a car. This is a great strategy to entice the dealer to do it.

I know you still have many questions like what about my trade in? What about financing, terms and interest rates? All this will be covered later.

"To successfully use my strategy you must negotiate the price of the new or used car you want, without bringing the trade or financing into the equation"

You may be thinking well how does this work? I have a trade and I want to finance. I understand that. Most deals will involve a trade in and 75% of all customers do take advantage of the dealership financing. **But in order for this strategy to work, you must concentrate on the new car price first.**

The dealership is trained to mix everything up together so that all they discuss with you is the payments, since ultimately that is what you are paying for the car. They use several different selling systems or worksheets designed to hide the price you are paying for the car, and your true trade allowance, and they never discuss interest rates or the term you are financing.

There is one very popular selling system dealerships still use today, called the "4 Square". This is simply a worksheet the salesperson pulls out that has lines at the top for all your current information, like name, address, phone number, your trade-in model, payoff information and who your lender is. Then instead of showing a running total of all the numbers, there are simply 4 large squares.

One square will say "List Price". Another square will say "Trade Allowance". The next square will say "Down Payment" and the last square will say "Monthly Payment". The trick to this type of selling system and I used the word trick, because that's what it is, is to keep you focused on the numbers that are written by the manager in those 4 boxes.

You never see a running total or breakdown of the numbers with the taxes or dealer fee, or the "out the door price", also known as the total amount you are financing.

The manager wants to keep you focused on only the number in these boxes.

If you say, I don't like what I'm getting for the trade-in he goes to the cash down and payments boxes.

It's designed to turn you into a "payment buyer". They will justify not showing you all the other numbers by saying "Mr. Customer, I understand you want to see all the numbers but since you are financing isn't the monthly payment what you are really paying for the car?" "So as long as I get the monthly payments in your budget range, all the other numbers should be in line".

When you get to the business office, the finance manager will go over all the details. You don't know what the term is, what the rate is, how much you are financing, you just know the payment range.

What if I told you customers fall for this every day? They will do all the paperwork, call their insurance company and switch coverage, move all their belongings to the new car, and they have no idea about the numbers that really matter!

If you allow the dealership to work your deal this way, you will lose. You must separate the new car price from the trade in amount, and then separate that from the financing. That is the purpose of this book. You have completed step one. You have successfully negotiated a loser deal for the dealer on the new car you want. **Now, and only now let's bring in the trade-in.**

Chapter 6

The Trade-In.

Everyone knows the object of the game is to get as much for your trade in as you can, while the dealership is trying to give you as little for your trade in as they can. **Dealerships are trained and skilled in the art of appraising a trade in.**

Most subscribe to expensive web based software that your "VIN" number or vehicle identification number is loaded into. The salesperson puts your "VIN" into the CRM computer software at his desk and that automatically loads into the used car manager's appraisal software.

This software tells the dealer how much your trade-in is selling for at the auctions, how much the car is in demand, what the average selling price of your trade-in is at other dealerships, how much money to deduct from the value for miles or damage or excessive wear and tear.

It tells them how fast this type of car sells, and so on. The salesperson has already done the silent walk around appraisal outside when you first arrived, remember? **So here is my strategy on how you get the most for your trade-in.**

"When the salesperson asks if that is your trade in, say you're not trading it in."

You already have it sold. Or you haven't thought about it. That will get the salesperson off the trade-in entirely and **now you can focus in on the new car purchase.**

Remember, **you must work each portion of the car deal separately** to get the best possible outcome. The dealer tries to avoid this, he wants to lump everything in together and come out with a monthly payment to try and close the deal. The less information he gives you, the more profit he makes.

Dealerships like to use the phrase "less is more" when working a car deal.

But now you have negotiated the best deal possible on the new car and it's time to see what the trade is worth. There are many advantages to trading your car into the dealership. One huge advantage is that it saves you money on sales tax since you only pay tax on the "difference" between the price of the new car and the amount of the trade in.

Take a $20,000 new car price minus $10,000 for your trade means you only pay sales tax on $10,000 which is the difference between the two numbers. Most states sales tax is around 7% so that's $700 in sales tax. But if you didn't trade your car in you would have to pay 7% of $20,000 which would be $1400 in tax.

You would pay an extra $700 in sales because you didn't have a trade-in. **A lot of educated people don't understand this.** And this isn't the only reason to use the dealership if possible to unload your trade.

Another great reason is you don't have to go to all the aggravation of advertising it on a website like Craigslist, which would mean you have to take time to meet strangers at your house or a mutual place to show off your car, which can dangerous and time consuming.

My experience has been a lot of these "tire kickers" don't even have the money to buy the car in the first place.

Also, if you have a payoff at the bank, or still owe money on the car, dealerships will pay that loan off immediately. If you try to sell your car on your own to a private buyer, most people are suspicious of handing a stranger, cash for a car and not getting a title.

The title is the official document registered with the state that proves ownership. They have to trust that you will take the money to the bank and pay the loan off. Then the title gets mailed to you (usually takes 30 days to get it) and you have to give it to the buyer.

In the meantime even though the buyer paid you for the car, he can't register the car without the title, so he is stuck for almost a month with a car he can't register and you have his money! Good luck.

Now sometimes there are circumstances when a customer has an inexpensive car and has the title with no liens, (meaning nothing is owed on the car) and then selling it on your own can be an advantage.

In the past this was true because new car dealerships didn't try to sell older model trades, for the simple reason that most banks won't finance an old car with a lot of miles. The dealership would simply take the car to the auction and hope to get what they put into it.

However, things have changed and new car dealers now are keeping more and more of the cheaper cars and selling them for cash, or are using sub-prime lenders or banks that specialize in financing poor credit customers on cheap cars with high miles.

My experience has been, the cheaper the car, the easier it is to sell to the public, and the more money you will get for it.

"You must do your homework on your trade to find its value before you bring it to the dealership"

This can be done many ways. A great way to do this is to first **have the car professionally detailed**. I have seen cars get as much as $500 extra in trade value just because it was shined up and clean. Then you can take the car to buying services like Carmax.

They will offer to buy your car and give you a hard cash 7 day offer to purchase your car. You may decide to not take the offer, but getting that first number is good to know.

Also, you can get your cars approximate value by visiting websites like Kelly Blue Book, or many other websites. You can also visit your local bank or credit union and they will give you a good idea of what your trade is worth. The best way to get the real value of your car is to simply take it to 2 different dealers. Let them give you a written appraisal for the car and between the two, come up with an acceptable number.

"Remember, buying a new car cannot be an impulse decision."

You have to be prepared. Let the impulse buyers that wander onto the lot and make a quick uninformed decision be the ones that the dealer makes a huge profit on. **That is better for you because if the dealer just make $6000 of the last customer he is more likely to take a "skinny or loser" deal off you.** I'm sorry but that's just the way it is.

No matter how many books are written, there will always be people that will overpay the dealer. They simply lack the knowledge you are receiving from this book. It's just the nature of the business. They will fall for some slick advertisement wander in "just to look" and "bing, bang, boom," 4 hours later they are riding away in a new car saying…

"I can't believe we bought a new car today, we only came in just to look!"That's the customer the dealer wants.

But you are not that customer, you understand that buying a car is the second largest purchase you will ever make, and it requires time and patience.

"You must be willing to get up and leave the negotiations at any time."

You cannot afford to get emotionally attached to the car. That's what the dealer wants. You are different because you are working your deal in parts, first the best price on the new car without the trade, then we are going to "sling the trade in". This is when you have finalized the price on the new car, and casually ask the salesperson, "say just curious what would you give me for my trade"?

"Dealers hate this".

The salesperson will go up to the desk and tell the manager, "Now they want to find out what the trade is worth". The desk manager is hot.

They understand that to get this deal now, not only did they have to lose money on the new car, but they have to give you a great number for your trade-in. **It's called going "wholesale to retail" in the car business.** This simply means that he can't sell you his car at wholesale meaning no profit and then give you retail for your trade-in.

No dealer wants to do this. He can't win. All his cards are on the table in plain view. He can't show you extra money for your car called "over allowance".

Over allowance is when the dealer works the deal off the addendum price. Let's say the addendum price is $24,997. Now let's also assume the rebates and incentives on the car are $1500.

The dealer has appraised your trade and determined it's worth $5000. You have no payoff on the car. Now the dealer has all the numbers to work your deal.

A good manager is going to only give you $3500 for your trade but, he is going to pencil the deal (this is when they take a marker pen and write all over the worksheet) and show you $5000 for your trade-in allowance with all rebates and incentives, and subtract that number from the addendum price (which you should never allow to happen) and come up with a difference of $19,997 plus tax, tag and title and (dealer fee which you should never pay). So what just happen?

The dealer made $1500 on your trade-in. He made around $2000 off the addendum sticker and he made another $1200 on the difference between what he paid for the car and the MSRP price, which totals around $4700 in profit plus his retro money and dealer cash.

Now the over allowance comes in when he has to discount the profit in his car (some of that $4700) and add it to your trade so it looks like he is giving you more for your trade than it is worth.

So remember the trade-in value is worth what the used car manager say's to put in the car. Anything you get over that amount is called "over allowance" and that money comes out of the dealers profit on the deal. You have a car appraised at $5000 and the dealer shows you $7000? Then that $2000 difference came out of his profit.

What if you are one of the few customers that actually have equity in your car? Another words, you owe less money to the bank than the car is worth. If you don't do your research to find out how much equity you could have, **the dealer will take it.** I have seen tons of customers come in on a "whim" unprepared, not realizing that they have equity in their trade-in. Most will have a "ballpark" idea of what their payoff is so if the dealer offers that amount, it sounds good to them! Really? What if you had $2000 in equity? See why it pays to be prepared?

If you use my strategy to buy your car, this won't happen to you. So let's assume you have gotten to this point by separating the deal, and first negotiating the price of the car you want to buy down to the bare minimum profit, if any.

So before the numbers come out the used car manager go out and appraises your **professionally detailed** trade-in. He comes back and looks in the computer to check the cars history and Carfax. This tells the manager if your car has ever been in an accident.

If it has, he will try to "de-value" your trade, telling you it's not worth what it should be because of the accident. Now the manager will send the salesperson back with a value for your trade-in. **Because he knows he is losing money on the price of the new car, he now will take the opportunity to "hold on the trade".**

That means to give you less than it's really worth. That way if he only gives you say $4500 for your car but it brings $6500 at the auction, he didn't lose money on your deal after all. He actually made money, or better yet, he puts the car on the lot, and retails it and makes even more.

So this portion of the negotiation is just as important as the one on the new car.

"I have done hundreds of deals and lost money on the new car only to make it up on the trade value "

Remember the elderly man with the Lexus trade in I told you about? I held $10,000 on his trade! Another words, I allowed him $10,000 less than it was really worth. He was unprepared, he didn't research his cars value, he was an impulse buyer and that happens every day in every dealership.

Don't be fooled into thinking that your hometown dealer would never do that to you.

"That is the nature of the business".

"Dealerships believe that they should make money off the ones they can, so it will make up for the ones they can't"

Luckily for you, you are prepared, you know what your car is worth, you have gotten several quotes and done some research, you are willing to trade the car in but only if you get the amount you want for the car.

Your leverage now is "Mr. Dealer, if I don't get what I want for my trade, I'm not buying your new car!' Wait a second, hold on did you just say I don't get my new car deal? That I have to call the detail department and tell them to stop cleaning your new car? That I'm not one deal closer to hitting my retro number for the month?

You get the picture. **You just won.** Everything is predicated on selling that new car. Dealers will switch customers from used cars to new cars just to hit that retro. It is the most important thing they do.

They have to keep the factory happy. You came in, very knowledgeable and negotiated a smoking great deal on a new car, they agreed to do the deal even though they are losing money, and now the whole thing is hinged on you getting top dollar for that old beater out there in the parking lot!

It's called "heads you win, tails you win more" either way you can't lose.

You don't have to worry with selling your car outside on the street. You got all the money you wanted for the car, and you saved money on the sales tax because you only pay tax on the difference!

Great job! Now let's discuss the rest of the process once the initial offer for your trade-in is made.

Say they come back and say, Mr. Customer, we are prepared to give you $5000 for your trade. Because you have done your research you think the car is worth $7000.

84.

How do you handle this? You don't negotiate. You simply stand up, say "thank you for your time" ask for your keys and slowly head to the door.

This will blow the salesperson's mind. The manager will run over because the strategically located receptionist called him and said you were standing up wanting your keys, the manager will say "hang on folks what's the problem I thought we had a deal already"?

He will sit down in the salespersons seat and get you to sit back down also. Go ahead. Simply explain that you thought you were buying a new car but don't like the amount for the trade. Explain that you wanted $7000 for your trade and were only offered $5000 (he knows all this by the way) and if you don't get $7000 you won't do business. At this point he is trained to be understanding and agreeable and disarming and his first counter offer will be to split the difference. This would be giving you $6000 instead of $5000 for the trade.

Some managers only like to go up in $300 increments because they know if they give up too much too fast, you will think there is a long way to go. I have only offered $100 extra, hundreds of times. You may take it you may not.

But remember **every dollar extra you get for your trade saves you sales tax.** So you offer to counter by splitting the difference again which would be getting you $6500 for your trade and with the sales tax savings you really would be getting almost $7000 which was your target number anyway so you have a deal. So what have we accomplished?

We take the number that we agreed to pay for the new car, subtract the $7000 and come out with a "difference" of let's say $15,000. Now on top of that you have to pay sales tax, and title fees, **BUT NOT THE DEALERS FEE.** This is where it gets slipped in there. Be careful to notice if any dealer fee has been added to the final price.

On a lot of dealers paperwork like the purchase agreement or buyers order, the amount is already hard printed on the form from the printing company, you need to scratch thru that. **No matter what the dealer says, you do not have to pay the dealers fee, it is a negotiable item.**

Some dealers don't charge a dealer fee at all, and advertise it everywhere they can. Others only have a small one of say $299. But just about every dealer in America has a dealer fee these days because it's pure profit and it adds up.

If they sell 150 cars a month that's around $120,000 in pure profit (based on a dealer fee of $799) that the salespeople are not paid on, only the managers and the Dealer. This is what the last dealer I worked for charged for a dealer fee.

Since we are discussing your trade-in, I think it's time to spend some detail on what "negative equity" is or as it is commonly referred to as being "upside down". **Typically because of the high price of cars today, 90% of all automobile purchases are financed with a bank.**

Now, understanding that **cars are not an appreciating asset,** the value of them drops each month because a new "black book" value is issued each month with the changes in value.

Even though there are many makes and models of cars, trucks and SUVs out there, I can assure you that no vehicles are "going up" in value when the next book comes out.

Cars are not like houses, where you can maintain them and keep them up, and make your payments and then a couple of years sell it for more than you paid for it.

Car values will not go up no matter what your do to the car. Your best hope is that your car only depreciates a little over time, taking into consideration that it has not been wrecked, or you have not put excessive miles on it. **These are killers to the value.**

If the Carfax says the car was in an accident and the airbags were deployed and vehicle had to be towed from the accident location, which it will say if it happened, then you are beat.

Your car is going to be worth far less than you expect because the dealer taking the car in on trade won't try to retail that car to another customer because if something with that car causes an accident, they can be sued for selling a car that has previously been wrecked, even though they disclosed it to the customer.

It will go straight to the auction, and the guys buying the cars at the auction, have a "VIN" scanner application on their phones that automatically runs the Carfax and gives them the value.

The auction itself will announce to the bidders that the car has frame damage or whatever. Even the auction buyers that desperately need used cars to sell will not bid much on these cars. I have seen instances where the Carfax is not correct on a car and by calling or emailing the company you can have some items deleted.

But if you get in an accident, and there is a police report that involves an insurance company, once it gets to the body shop for repair, it gets reported to Carfax.

I know of people that will fix the car themselves and pay a body shop without going through insurance just so the damage doesn't get on the Carfax.

But back to negative equity. Normally on a standard 60 month loan, if you take good care of your car and only put the allowed miles (12,000) per year, you can plan to break even around 40 months. **That means that the value of the car is equal with what you owe the bank to pay the car off.** This rarely happens for many reasons.

A lot of customers get bored with the car they have and want to trade it sooner, before they have caught up with the negative equity, or they had negative equity on the car they traded to get the car they have now and it was rolled into the new loan, making the payoff or amount financed a lot more than it should be, making the payoff higher.

Also less and less customers are putting a sizable cash down payment on a car these days, because they see all the "Zero down delivers" ads we talked about. Just about **all customers in a lease are severely upside down** until almost the maturity date of their lease. We will cover more on leasing later. So understanding negative equity is imperative to not overpaying for your next car.

"A good rule of thumb is every $1000 financed equals $20 a month in payments".

So, if you are seeking a $300 a month payment, based the above formula you must be financing no more than $15,000 (based on a decent interest rate and 60 months financing).

Most customers are surprised to find out that they owe more on their car that the dealership is willing to offer them.

The only option available to offset this difference is the put "money down".

Now understand, depending on your credit score (more on Credit Scores later) and how "buried" you are, most banks will finance the next car purchase and allow you to "roll the negative equity" into the new loan. The more money you put down, the lower the payments.

Dealerships have also been forced to extend the terms of the loan to compensate for the rise in the price of cars because people would not be able to afford the payments.

The standard finance term now is 72 months, but I did some 84 month loans recently and it's only available to customers with perfect credit. But keep in mind, the longer you finance the car, the longer you have to keep it to catch up with the negative equity. We will spend more time on the finance terms later in the financing portion of the book. So now you should have a better understanding of negative equity and the importance of getting all you can for your trade, because that will reduced the negative equity you would have to roll into the next loan.

"It is nothing these days to see customers $7000 to $12,000 upside down in their existing cars"

Usually, they are shocked and surprised that they can't trade without serious money down like ($5000) or don't understand why their new payment is going up an extra

$300 a month! You may you be asking yourself "well how do I avoid this negative equity problem"?

Don't overpay the dealer by letting him make a huge profit!

Also, when you buy the car with my system, you are "in the new car right" meaning that you bought the car at or below what the dealer paid for the car so the depreciation hit won't affect you as much.

Also try to avoid financing the car for longer than you need to, the shorter the term the quicker you build equity, and the less you pay in interest over the life of the loan. The payments will be higher the shorter the term you go, you have to get all the options on how much the payment goes down by extending the term according to your budget.

Also, most customers in equity when they trade cars have cash or trade equity to put into the new car deal and that lowers the amount financed on the car.

All of these help, along with taking good care of your trade, watching the miles, and stay away from accidents even though they are not your fault! The Carfax report does not say whose fault caused the accident, only that your vehicle has been wrecked and repainted etc.

So now, let's recap what we learned in this trade-in section of the book.

1. Do your homework on your trade-in. Get several offers to buy from several different sources/dealers.
2. Search the internet and go to websites that will value your car like KBB.com.
3. Have your trade professionally detailed and fix important items like the A/C etc.
4. Bring the trade discussion up ONLY AFTER you have negotiated the best price of the new car.
5. Be prepared to leave and not buy the new car if you don't get the price you want for your trade.
6. During the negotiations, respond to their offer by splitting the difference between their last offer and what you want.
7. Remember that the dealership is probably the best place to trade in your car instead of selling in the street because you save money on the sales tax.
8. Know what your pay off is if you have a loan remaining on your car, you may have equity in your trade-in.

<u>Chapter 7</u>

<u>Financing: the Hidden Killer.</u>

So you have picked out your new car, negotiated the best price by using the show me the invoice strategy, agreed on a fair price for your trade in, not agreeing to pay the dealer fee, and now you have to determine which route you will take on the financing of your purchase, **will you finance with the dealer?**

Use your own private bank or credit union? Or pay cash.

We will cover the advantages of all these options but first let's discuss how the Dealership financing department works.

Back in the early 70s dealers started to figure out that the price of their new cars was climbing higher and higher. In the old days, the customer would pay for the car by going to their own bank or paying cash.

Dealers figured out that if they could get someone to finance the car while they had the customer at the dealership, not only would they get the sale right then, but there would be an opportunity to make a couple of bucks off the financing and some extra products.

Hence, the F&I department was created with a full time dedicated finance manager to run the show. Over the years the F&I departments in dealerships have evolved into a major profit source for the dealer.

> **"I have worked in dealerships that generate over $250,000 a month in F&I department profits."**

Most customers have completely let their guard down when they are taken into the finance department and a little overwhelmed from the negotiation process they just went thru. The dealership knows this.

The finance manager will calmly come over and congratulate you on your purchase at the salespersons desk and say **"I will be assisting you in finalizing all your paperwork and you will be on your way".**

Again **you have to treat this like a separate transaction** just like we did on the new car purchase price negotiations and then again on the trade value negotiations. Don't for a second let your guard down, because you are far from out of the woods. The finance manager is a trained professional assassin. Sorry, but it's just the way it is. He does not make a dime for himself off the profit on the sale of the car. (Hopefully you didn't let them make any). His sole purpose in life is to sell you his finance products and make reserve profit.

Reserve profit is any extra interest the dealer can charge you over and above the best rate you qualified from the bank. For instance, say you have a decent credit score, and the desk managers submitted your application to 4 lenders to get the best rate possible. Let's say Bank A came back with a buy rate of 2.99%. Each state is different, but in Florida the Dealer can mark up that interest rate as much as 2% points.

So instead of offering you the buy rate of 2.99% they figure your payment and the finance manager will tell you the rate will be 4.99%. Now you might be thinking "well that doesn't sound like a whole lot of money" but hang on.

Let's say you are financing the average amount now on a new car in today's market which is around $25,000. 2% extra on the interest rate over the amount of the term of 72 months is around $2000. Wow, **the Dealer just made $2000 in profit off you to offset all the good negotiating you did on the purchase of the new car and the value of your trade.**

I have seen it done thousands of times. Customers just lay down. Why? Because they are uneducated and under prepared. They don't know what interest rate their credit score qualifies them for therefore they don't realize the rate the dealership charged them has been marked up. If you ask the Dealer "is this best rate I can get"? They will say absolutely. **And it is simply not true. It's negotiable, just like everything else.**

"You could have gotten a better interest rate; they just don't want to give it to you"

And that's because they stand to make a killing off the reserve profit. I can't tell you how many times a day this happens in every dealership in America. You have to be informed and educated or the dealer will make money off the reserve every time. Even if he only makes 1% extra in rate, it is still profit to the dealer and drives up the payoff of your car loan.

You must understand the interest charges are figured into the payoff amount you owe on the car. That means the higher the interest rate, the higher the payoff amount. This contributes to the negative equity cycle we discussed in the last chapter.

"Customers pay more interest than they have to 90% of the time".

You may be reading this and thinking…**my hometown Dealer would never do that to me, don't believe it.** I have worked in small town dealerships and large metro marker dealerships and they all have a finance department and this is how they get paid.

The Finance manager keeps a running log for the month in his desk or on the computer that at any time will show how much money he has generated for the month just in reserve profit.

Why do you think the dealer is so set on doing the financing for you and not letting you go to your own bank? That's right, the reserve profit. Not that your own bank won't do the same thing the only difference is they won't try to make the maximum allowed by the state. I have worked in states that had NO cap on how much the dealer could overcharge on the interest rate!

> **"It was common place to see $4000 to $5000 profit just off the interest rate".**

So how do you combat this technique? You have to be prepared and do your homework. Don't be the impulse emotional buyer we previously talked about that just buys a car and had no plan to. That's who the dealer wants. **He wants you to be uneducated.**

Here are a couple of things you can do to be prepared to win this battle. Go to your local bank where you do business, even if you have not financed a car there and fill out a loan application and find out what your credit score is and what kind of rates they offer on the car you want. You can also do this online.

Your credit score all determine your interest rate. Credit unions rates are usually lower for their members than local banks. You just have to check it out, it's important.

If you don't know what your score is, and what rate you can get, you will not know where the bottom is. You will have to take the dealers word for it and that's what they want.

Now it is important to discuss the special financing incentives that are sometimes offer by the dealer and the manufacturer. These are the "Zero Percent" financing ads you see on TV or in the paper. They do exist and are real.

However, when you get to the dealership and inquire about the 0% rate you find out the "real deal". In most cases you can only get that rate on specific cars the manufacturer wants the dealer to sell.

All the major manufacturers have their own finance banking institutions owned by them and they are called the "captive lenders" The dealership is encouraged and incentivized to use the captive lenders anytime they sell a car. The factory banks are the ones giving out the 0% so that you will buy a car. No other bank or credit union would do this because they don't make any money giving it out for 0%.

The factory bank is willing to do this only if you buy the car they want you to buy, agree to the term they want you to take (usually 36 to 60 months) and agree to forfeit some rebate money you would have received in lieu of taking the 0%. This is how this works, let's say manufacturer ABC wants to sell his slow moving SUV product.

He places a rebate or customer cash on this vehicle of $2000. Or he offers the 0% financing option but both are displayed on the TV screen when you see the commercial. It's only when you get to the dealership do they disclose that it's either or.

You don't get both. So you have to decide which one comes out in your favor by doing some simple math. For instance, let's say you have excellent credit, and your bank already offered you 1.9%.

Then depending on the term you want to finance and how much you are financing you need to decide if the 0% is better even though you now lose the $2000 in factory rebates. It's fairly simple to calculate.

Financing $15,000 at 0% for 60 months would cost you zero. But what if you took the $2000 in rebates from the dealer and financed the car with your bank at 1.9% over the same term?

Now you are only financing $13,000 but at a rate of 1.9% not 0% (because you took the $2000 rebate you don't get the 0% also). **In most cases 0% is hard to beat, it's free money.** But you need to run the numbers both ways to find out which is the best option.

"If you take the 0% option, don't put any money down!"

Why would you? It's free money! Your cash down payment left in the bank will draw some interest so why pull it out to put it down on a loan with 0% financing.

So you need to be aware of the advantages and disadvantages of these offers. The dealer doesn't want you to take the 0% offer why? Because he can't make any finance profit off the interest rate! He will always try to get you finance the most money possible because he knows the more money you finance the more reserve profit he makes if he is allowed to markup the rate.

Even in the rare occasion that he actually gives you the best rate you qualify for and doesn't mark it up he receives a check from the lender he uses called a "flat" and usually depending on how much you finance can be around $400.

You can ask the dealer if he is getting a "flat commission" from the lender and ask for that money to be taken off the amount financed. The finance manager will be stunned just by the fact that you know about the "flat" and will say he cannot do that, simply stand up in his office and say "thank you for his time" and he will promptly remove himself to go get permission from the manager.

"Remember this, once you are in the finance office they will do anything to make sure the deal gets done"

100.

You have all the power. I have had to go into the finance office hundreds of times and give away this or that just to get the customer to sign up and not let the deal "unwind".

If by using this book the only thing you took away was the education to ask for the finance flat commission amount which is around $400 then you made out! Trust me when I say no one knows about this industry "insider information". And the ones that do don't want you to know about it.

"You are truly getting secret insider dealership information that very few buyers knows about "

There is no way that you would know unless you worked in a dealership. Even most of the salespeople don't know what I just showed you. They are kept in dark as much as possible because they will discuss it with the customer and that's what the dealership doesn't want to happen.

So let's recap what we have learned regarding the interest rate.

1. Do your own research and find out about your credit score.
2. Find out what outside lending institutions will charge you for interest.
3. Understand that the dealer is marking up the rate as much as 2% points.
4. Ask the dealer to put in writing that this is the best rate available. (He won't)
5. Do the math to see if the 0% option is best vs giving up the rebate money.
6. If the dealer is using the best buy rate ask if he is getting a "flat commission" from the lender.
7. Do your homework, remember knowledge is power.
8. Don't relax in the finance office, serious profit is made there.

Ok, so here's what the typical experience is like when you are seated in the business office. You are comfortably and strategically placed in an area where the finance manager has everything he needs to make money. First off, remember when he came out to introduce himself and say he would be ready for you shortly? That is all trained.

He wants to put you at ease. You know him now so when you arrive in his office you are not alarmed.

But more importantly, he wants the time it takes to go back into his office and begin printing all the documents (around 30) that you will be signing that have nothing to do with the products he will try to sell you or the actual bank contract.

He can't print that yet because he doesn't know what interest rate you will agree to or what extra products you will buy. All this information goes on the bank contract. So when you initially get seated he will already have a huge stack of documents in a stack upside down to his right printed out and ready to be signed.

He will begin by nonchalantly sliding these documents in front of you one by one for your signature. This is by design. Remember nothing is left to chance in a dealership.

He presented himself as someone that is going to finalize your paperwork. He doesn't want to look like he is selling anything. **Everything is rehearsed and he has learned his trade by being videoed and critiqued**. He wants to get you in the mood to be comfortable signing your name.

He will place insignificant documents in front of you like, "this is to transfer your tag" please ok here, "this is to pay off your trade" please ok here, "this is to apply for your title", please ok here etc.

All this is planned to get you in the signing mood so that when he slides the important documents that **he gets paid on,** you will be programmed to keep on signing. I can say this, government documents like your tag and title work fees ARE NOT marked up, neither is the sales tax amount you pay.

Dealers are always concerned about audits and 99% of the legal problems they encounter involve what happens in the business office. I recently ran a dealership where the dealer videotaped the entire process in the finance office. That way if the customer came back and said "I never agreed to this" or "I wasn't told I was paying for that" he has it all on video.

But this is rare, very few dealers do this because they are afraid of what can be done by the finance manager, and they don't want it on video. So let's get into the profit opportunities that await the unsuspecting customer that strolls into the business office.

"As I said, once your seated everything is planned and rehearsed."

After the business manager has you sign around 10 documents that are basic information he is ready to present the "MENU". The menu is simply a hard printed piece of paper with several different options on it for you to review. Remember how I told you that Dealers want to sell you a car with as little information as possible? Like not telling you the selling price or trade value? And only quoting you payments because that's what you are paying for the car? Well this is why.

You must understand that when the sales manager quotes you a payment on the showroom floor, he will typically add $20 to sometimes $80 dollars a month to the payments that you see. This is called "Leg". Why does he do this? Because he wants to leave room for the finance manager to add in his products all the while your payments didn't go up.

This is sometimes referred to "payment packing" and is illegal in some states. It used to be done on a regular basis but recent lawsuits and legislation has curbed this technique to some degree. But it still goes on today in a lot of dealerships and you need to be aware of it.

When the payments are presented on the showroom floor by the salesperson by the manager, they will have a range of say $340s-$380s a month. This is the "leg".

If you ask why is there is such a difference or disparity in the payments the sales manager is trained to say "Well Mr. Customer, the business manager has the computer that is connected to the bank and he will get your payments closer to the penny, mine just gives a range on the payments, but it's no problem he will go over all that with you shortly". That was pretty smooth huh?

"Well that payment spread just made the dealership $1000 for every $20 you agree to in extra payments!"

Remember the math? Every $1000 is $20 a month increase on your payments. Now assuming that you were set up with the payment leg and have no idea as to what your payments are exactly, the finance manager will present the "menu" with Option A, B, C and D. Option "A" is simply the total price you are financing with the number of months and the interest rate.

Option "B" is the same as "A" but they have added an extended warranty contract which runs the payments up about $30 a month.

They don't disclose the total price of the warranty yet, they only show how much the payments are going up. Why do they do this? Because **something that only cost you $30 extra dollars a month sound a lot better than $1895 right?** If they just blurted that price out most customers would pass.

A good finance manager will sell over 60% of the customers he sees an extended service contract. It normally has around $800 to $1000 profit built in. Again hidden profit to the Dealer. And guess what the best part is?

"The Dealer actually owns the warranty company the backs the extended warranty"

That's right, every dime of that $1895 goes into an account that is owned by the dealer and the dealer pays a company to simply administer the warranty paperwork and oversee claims. It's a massive profit center for the dealer.

So let's discuss whether or not the extended warranty is worth buying. By now you should be getting a picture of all the ways the dealer can make money on you even if they lose money on the sale of the new or used car. "

"It's just like a casino, the longer you stay the odds lean to the house, and the house always wins"

So is the extended warranty worth buying? Well let's see. First off, all new cars come with at least 2 free warranties. Most have the 3 year or 36,000 mile bumper to bumper warranty backed by the factory. This warranty is good at any of the manufacturer's dealerships in the country.

It absolutely covers everything on the car except normal maintenance oil changes etc. It's bulletproof. And since most customers today trade their cars every 3 years it's usually all the warranty you will need. The same new car also comes with a 5 year or 60,000 power train warranty.

This only covers the engine, transmissions and major components of the vehicle, but again, a good warranty and it came with the car at no additional charge. Also keep in mind that these warranties from the factory have a $0 deductible, so you never have to come out of pocket. Also if you try to trade the car in while the car still has some of this factory warranty remaining, it is transferable to the next owner so the car has more value on trade in.

Also as I am writing this book, **several import manufacturers now offer a 10 year 100,000 warranty on their new cars free of charge!**

There are some limitations for instance, like its only good to the original owner but still, it's a great warranty. So why do 60% of customers STILL BUY THE EXTENDED WARRANTY? **Because of the way it is presented.** The finance manager will ask you a series of questions like how long do you keep your vehicles?

How many miles a year will you drive? Have you ever had to pay for any major repairs before? He will show you a recent repair bill from the service department where some poor soul paid $3800 for a transmission.

He will also tell you the extended is transferable and cancellable so if you ever trade the car in or sell it, you can get back a portion of the money you paid for it you haven't used. This is true.

"But 90% of the customers that buy the extended warranty never use it."

They trade the car in before it is needed or sell the car within a couple of years of buying it. Remember the

extra money for this warranty gets added to the total amount of money you are financing which contributes to negative equity.

The warranty is presented in a way that makes you think it's only a few extra dollars a month, the price of a nice lunch each month will pay for the wonderful warranty. If you decline to purchase the warranty, they make you sign a form declining coverage, which is designed to make you feel stupid for not wanting it.

"My best advice to you is to not buy the extended warranty".

Keep in mind even if you are the rare customer that keeps his car till "the wheels fall off" once you buy the car, over the next few years you will be bombarded with offers in the mail to buy a extended warranty for your car.

Especially, when these companies see that your factory warranty is about to run out. Also you can simply return to the dealership when your factory warranty is about to run out and purchase an extended warranty from the finance manager at that time.

He will be happy to stop what he is doing and sell you a warranty, remember he gets paid on the profit. Also, since the Dealer owns the extended warranty company, the people that are paid to run the warranty company are trained to reject a lot of the warranty claims you may have. They will say you didn't perform the scheduled recommended factory maintenance on the car, so the warranty is voided and so on.

All this is in the fine print on the back of the warranty agreement. And if they do approve the warranty claim, you will have to pay a deductible of around $100 for each repair. An extended warranty is like an insurance claim.

They have done all the studies and know your repairs will never use up the $1895 that was put in their pockets, not to mention the fact that you are paying interest on this money because it was added into the total amount you financed. In the state of Florida extended warranties are considered insurance products and are regulated by the state. Finance managers are not allowed to discount the warranties the price is non negotiable.

But since he can't discount the warranty, he can extend the term on your car loan which would make the payments on the car lower. That would leave more budget room for the warranty and make him some more interest rate profit, since the longer you finance the car the more interest profit is generated.

Some other states may or may not do this so if you really want to buy the extended warranty, try to negotiate the price. It doesn't hurt to try. **But again I do not recommend you buy the warranty.**

The Dealer would not be selling it to you if he wasn't making money off it. That brings us to Option "B" of the menu. This option will include the price of the car plus the extended warranty plus gap insurance and wheel and tire protection. Again, these products are massive profit centers for the Dealer. Gap insurance however can be a viable product.

Here's how it works, if you finance a car for say $20,000 and get into a accident, and the car is totaled meaning a total loss, most insurance companies will only pay you back for the value of the car, not taking into consideration what you owe on the car. It's not their business. They don't care what you owe only what it is worth.

So a lot of customers will have a deficiency balance between how much the insurance is giving them and what they owe on the car hence the "gap". Sounds good huh? The gap insurance steps in pays the difference. Well sometimes it does. However, I have seen instances when the difference was so great that the gap insurance will only pay up to a certain limit.

Many customers are left to continue making payments on a car they no longer can drive. I'm not saying gap insurance is not worth buying. It depends on the type of vehicle it is. High line import cars sometimes present good reasons to buy gap insurance. If you really want it, **you can buy it cheaper from your local insurance agent.**

Most sell gap to their customers for a lot less than the dealer and you don't have to include it in your auto loan and pay interest on it. Also, these days most manufactures that have their own financing companies like Nissan Motor Acceptance include Gap Insurance for free when you lease a car.

As for options "C" and "D" don't even waste your time. These options include all the products we previously discussed plus a couple more (varies by dealership) but here is a quick list.

Wheel and tire protection. This covers you in case you damage a rim or get a flat tire. It is not worth the cost of around $499. You can take a rim to a good body shop and have it touched up for less than $50.Your tires have a warranty and an AAA membership for around $50 will cover towing and some other expenses. Also a lot of manufacturers today give you road side assistance free. **Don't buy it.**

Glass Etching. This is where the Dealer has a company come out and etch a long numeric series of numbers into every window of the car at the very bottom and hardly noticeable. The pitch is that if your car is stolen and chopped up they can still identify your car by the window etching code. This product is worthless and out of date. **Don't buy it.**

GPS Tracking Devices. This is another product that offers protection by allowing you to log onto a website and locate the precise location of your car at any time. Sounds good, but you can do the same thing with your cell phone for free.

My iphone has a locate function and at any time I can see where all the phones on my account are located. Again, the dealer wouldn't offer it if he didn't profit from it. **Don't buy it.**

Paint Sealant & Fabric Protector. This product promises to repair blemishes in your paint due to acid rain, or fading, or bird droppings or love bug damage and also repair the interior from rips or tears. It also cleans the interior from grape juice stains or blemishes or fading.

First off, your new car has a factory warranty on the paint free of charge, and you have to have a car for several years before you need to be worried about worn out spots or holes in the interior.

This normally cost around $599 and my experience has been that when a customer wanted to use it fix a hole in the seat or whatever, it was due to an issue caused by the customer and not covered.

You can visit your local auto parts store and buy a can of "Scotchguard" and spray your interior and it will give you the same protection. I can't tell you how many times I had to stop what I was doing and handle a complaint from a customer that was sorry he purchased these products. **Don't buy it.**

Rustproofing and Undercoating. This product offers to have the dealer service department spray a protective coating under your car to prevent rust or damage and improve noise reduction. You don't need it. Today's new cars are manufactured with good corrosion protection. **Don't buy it.**

This pretty much covers the extra products the finance manager is paid to sell you. Again, the total cost of these products are figured into the monthly payments so if you were sent into the finance office with a payment "range" with a $40 a month spread, and already agreed to the payments, all the business manager has to do is disclose these products and your payments come out "around" where the sales manager told you.

If you know exactly what the payment is based on the total amount you are financing which I suggest you should know, some quick math will tell you how much this stuff cost. I will say that each product you do decide to buy will have its own separate contract, and you will have to sign it to accept coverage.

If you look closely the full amount of the product is printed on the page. But because the finance manager has you programmed to quickly sign away your name and he slides the form away, most customers don't know what the total cost is until they get home or open up their paperwork weeks or months later.

Now, on your actual bank contract, the main document you sign, showing all the figures and payments, there is a place to see what the total of all the extra products you purchased costs you. The finance manager is trained to go over this document with you in a clever fashion.

He won't say this is your bank CONTRACT, because that word is scary and binding. He will use the word AGREEMENT which sound much more agreeable. He won't say "I need your SIGNATURE on this form" because that sound too legal and binding but simply "please put your OK here, here, and also here". See? Like I have been saying all along,

"Everything that is done at the Dealership is for a reason and not by chance"

People who have not read this book or ever worked in a dealership are in no way prepared for the processes and procedures that are in place to separate you from your money! They simply don't stand a chance. Sure they can shop around and say they have bought many cars over the years, (I used to love these customers) but they are no match for the professional dealership employees.

"So my advice to you is to read over your bank contract line by line".

Finance managers **hate this**. They will even place their hand over certain areas to cover numbers they don't

want you to see, when they are showing you where to put your OK. But don't be pressured. This is the most important document you will ever sign because it is legal and binding. Once you sign that document and drive that car off the lot you are "done". You have legally taken possession of the vehicle.

That's why the Dealer wants you to drive it off the lot. If you sign all the documents and leave the dealership without driving the new car off the lot, you can still cancel the transaction. You haven't legally taken delivery. Dealers know this.

So when customers say well "I want to go home and empty out my car and come back and pick up the new car" the managers will not let that happen. They will say "go ahead and take the new car, we will have the salesman follow you home with your trade in, and you can unload the car, and he can bring it back".

That is because they know you legally took the car "over the curb" and now it's done. I have seen many instances where the customer signed everything, went through the business office, but left in their own car for whatever reason, and then changed their minds and never came back to pick up the car. No matter how many times the dealer calls you and threatens you, he is beat.

You never legally took delivery and a good lawyer will get you out every time. But we will cover this more in detail

later under (Pressure tactics). So let's get back to the bank contract.

First make sure the amount you are financing (usually line 3) on the contract is the number that you negotiated out front with the manager. Assuming you don't buy any additional products from the finance manager (which I told you not to do) this number should jive. Then look towards the top.

You will see several boxes with APR% that's your annual percentage rate. This is the interest rate we discussed earlier. Make sure it's exactly the same as you negotiated. The next block will have the total of payments.

This is where the total amount of your monthly payment times the number of months you are financing or the term are multiplied to show what the car will cost you over the life of the loan after all the payments are made.

Again, I cannot stress enough the importance of looking this contract over with due diligence. Take your time, the longer the better. Remember, in most states there is no 3 day return policy.

Most customers are under the "delusion" that they have 3 days to return the car for any reason and as I said earlier, especially in Florida that is not the case. Customers will bring up the "lemon law act" and say I can return this car as long as I bring it back in 3 or 7 days. Not So.

First off, the lemon law act passed by the government has nothing to do with buyer's remorse or changing your mind because you can't afford the payment, or your wife yelled at you for buying a car without talking to her.

The Lemon Law Act is something that involves a factory defect with the car you bought, and after many visits to the service department because your new car won't operate properly, you can get another car in substitution from the factory and sent to the Dealer.

It is very rare and I have only seen it done maybe 5 times in 25 years of being in the car business. So don't get the two issues confused. Know what you are signing and the implications involved.

In most cases, **"Once you sign everything and drive the car off the lot, it's yours."**

In today's world of technology and internet options, your new car is already registered in your name by the state in which you live by the time you leave the dealership.

Depending on the manufacturer the Dealer can "e-contract" which means electronically submit the contract to the bank to get his money the same day you bought the car.

This is important because it helps the Dealer control his cash flow. In the old days Dealers used to have to gather all the documents you signed together in a huge packet and mail them to the back that approved your loan.

The bank would look over the deal and look for any mistakes or discrepancies like "scratch outs" or the customer signed in the wrong place and would send the paper work back to the Dealer without sending him a check.

Dealerships watch this very closely and even run a daily report for all the managers to see called the "CIT" or "contracts in transit" report. This tells them all the contracts or deals that are floating around and they have not gotten paid for the car.

Remember earlier, the Dealers don't own the cars to begin with, they took out a loan to place the cars on their lot, and they are paying interest on that loan, so the longer it sits, or isn't paid off, the more interest they pay.

That's why if you've ever bought a car and the dealership called you to come back in and resign some documents, a mistake was made either by them or by you and they need it fixed to get paid for the car by the bank. Now if this ever happens to you and during the period you have had the car you wished you hadn't bought it or wished you could return it, this is your chance!

"Because.. if you don't resign the new paperwork the dealer will never get paid."

I have seen customers come back to resign and tell the Dealer they didn't want the car, and the Dealer would drop the price or lower the payments or throw in a free warranty, of whatever they have to do finalize the deal. The dealer is in too deep now with your deal to "unwind" it.

Chances are he has already reported the car sold to the manufacturer called "punching the RDR" or retail delivery report. All dealers usually do this within a couple days of you buying a new car.

That lets the factory know you sold the car and they keep running totals for the month to see how the Dealer is progressing towards his "retro" number for the month. Remember that?

He has also probably sold your trade at auction and can't or won't produce it. Sometimes he has already paid off your trade-in loan with your bank.

Normally however, most dealers don't pay off your car till they get funded or paid on the new car, and customers come in all the time mad because they got a call saying a payment was due or late on the trade and it was going to show up on their credit report. This is common place and most of time you can call the dealer and get it resolved.

But understanding your options and the ramifications of signing everything and taking the car are imperative to your knowledge and preparation before you arrive at the dealership.

Now we didn't cover the occasion where you are not using the dealership financing and have agreed to finance the car with you own bank. This makes a HUGE difference in the amount of time you will spend in the business office.

First off, a good finance manager will try to convert you to dealership financing by asking what type of interest rate you are getting and that if he could match it or beat it, would you finance with the dealership? Why would he offer to do this?

"Because he knows he has a greater chance to sell his products if he can include them in your payments"

Plus even if he gives you his best rate remember he still gets the "flat" commission from the bank. So basically, it all comes down to whether he can provide the financing for you and then present the menu or whether you are simply writing a check for the car.

If you are paying cash for the car he will then have to "step sell" his products which is hard to do because you will have to add the price of his products to the amount you were going to write the check for. Most customers won't do this.

"Now you know why dealerships try so hard to do the financing for you"

Another reason they want to do the financing and not have you write them a check is because checks can have "stop payments" placed on them, customers can change their minds and simply stop payments on their check and the Dealer has a problem.

But if the dealer does the financing all is done and he can control the deal better PLUS sell you extra products.

"Dealerships actively track their finance penetration or what percentage of their cars sold are financed by the dealership" They have meetings every month with all the finance managers to review their performance and see how many products per retail deal they are selling called their "PVR".

"A good finance manager will average over $1500 in profit on the products he sells on each car sold"!

They should average around 70%. They will try to convert you to dealership financing by using several cash conversion closing techniques on you.

Here is one very effective one. Say, you are financing your new car at your ABC credit union. The finance manager will agree that the credit union is a great place to do business. He may even say he is a member of the credit union himself.

Then he will say "Mr. Customer, wouldn't you agree that if you ever need money for a loan for emergencies or a vacation or whatever, the credit union is the best place to go"?

You would usually agree and nod your head. He will then ask, "wouldn't you also agree that there is a limit to how much money any one person can borrow"? You would nod your head, yes. Then he will say "that's why 99% of our customers let the dealership take care of financing the car for them".

"You see Mr. Customer, the credit union is the best and easiest place to get an emergency loan, all you have to do is go down there and sign a few papers because let's face it they know you".

"But since we all have a limit as to how much any one lending institution will lend us, what would happen if you financed this new car at your credit union. This is around $25,000. You would have just reduced the amount of easy money you can borrow for emergencies or whatever by $25,000.".

"This would make it difficult to borrow any more money for something else you may need in a time of emergency, or when you wanted to take a vacation".

"Again, that's why most of our customers will finance the car at the dealership and still have their line of credit available at the credit union in case they need it, from the easiest place to borrow it. I mean why put all your eggs in one basket? Sounds pretty good huh? It works too. People will say ok what is your rate?

124.

The business manager will ask you what rate you have at the credit union and then go to work. He will either get you a lower rate and mark it up to just below what your credit union was giving or match it and get his "flat" commission.

Best of all he gets a chance to sell you all his products and include them in your payments which make them much easier to sell. Pretty slick huh? I was a finance manager for 6 years and used this conversion tactic to perfection.

Here is a good cash conversion tactic. If you are simply paying cash and there is no lien being placed on the car they will offer up the "Zero Percent" loan.

They will say "Mr. Customer, why would you take your hard owned money out of the bank or out of an IRA or money market account where you are drawing some interest on your money, when you can leave you cash where it is to keep drawing interest and borrow the money for our bank at 0%"? Actually this is pretty smart.

I mean 0% is hard to beat. Plus with all lending institutions these days you can pay off the loan early with no pre payment penalty. Another great feature but that can be done at your own bank as well.

Also a lot of retired customers have to pay penalties to take money out of IRAs or money market accounts, or even 401ks. Again, 0% will sound awful good.

So by now you should have some valuable information when you sit down in the finance office. Remember everything is done to make a profit off of you.

"Don't feel sorry for the dealership, they will make all the money they need off the impulse emotional buyers".
Don't let that be you!

Chapter 8

The Importance of Understanding Your Credit

Your credit score controls all of your major purchases today. So in order to be fully educated on the car buying process, you need to have a clear understanding of your credit and **how it is used against you at the dealership.** Many years ago credit "scores" did not exist. This is also known as the "FICO" index.

In the old days, if you wanted credit to buy a car or whatever, you simply filled out a reference sheet with some names and numbers of people or businesses that offered you credit in the past. The dealer and his banks would call these references and find out if you were "credit worthy".

Then a small company in Atlanta, Georgia called **Equifax,** opened up and put this credit information into a standardized report form. This form showed not only how you paid, but what accounts you had opened, how much you owed, what the payment amounts are, if you have ever been over 30, 60, or 90 days late. If you ever defaulted on a loan, and how many places you applied for credit.

All this data is still the basis of what goes into your credit report today. The only difference now is, you have a total "score" assigned to your credit report.

This score was originally designed to tell lenders or banks what the probability was of your filing for bankruptcy. That's right, that's all they wanted to know. And the more open accounts you had, will balances remaining, combined with how many times you applied for loans and how you paid those loans, generate your "score" or bankruptcy probability.

Today, everything is based off your credit score. Everywhere you apply for credit, the only thing that comes up is your score. Most places where you apply for credit like to open a bank account, or lease an apartment don't even see your total credit report. They only get your score.

Scores vary from people that have no credit, like students or first time buyers, to people with years of credit and several different types of loans on their credit reports. If you have never had credit, what we referred to as a "ghost", you would have a credit score of 0.

This score simply means you have not had a chance to get out there and build credit. Typically students, or recent college graduates, (which car lenders love) and people that pay cash for everything, will have a 0 credit score.

These people can get financing for a car under certain circumstances. Most of the time they are young adults trying to get started and the bank will require a co-signer.

A co-signer is usually a relative like a parent or spouse. They typically have good established credit and they are basically guaranteeing the loan. If the person or the person with the 0 beacon defaults on the loan, the bank will make the co-signer responsible for the payments due.

It's a huge responsibility but it's done every day. The next big jump in credit scores will be from 0 to around 425. A 425 is pretty much the lowest credit score a person can have.

The best score hovers around the 850 range. So depending on how you pay your bills, your score is somewhere in between. The 425 usually cannot buy a car. They will have several repossessions, unpaid utility bills, late payments on everything they have, and typically late or past due on the car they have now.

A lot of these customers can sometimes get approved but the bank will require a huge down payment. Like $6000 to $8000. The average credit score in America today is around 670. This customer can usually buy whatever they want, as long as they have the income to justify the purchase.

Let's talk about that. Banks have a maximum amount a car payment can be based on someone's income. This is called the "PTI" or payment to income.

A good rule of thumb is whatever your monthly income is your maximum payment cannot exceed 15% of that

amount. So if you make $3000 a month, your maximum car payment allowed is around $450. Customers with credit scores above the 750 range usually don't have to worry about the "PTI" the banks will "waive" this rule because they want their business.

So understanding what your score is and how it affects your ability to purchase a car is paramount to getting a decent car loan. By law you are allowed 1 free credit report per year.

There are many websites that offer that service. Most banks will have a "tier system" for determining what interest rate you will pay for your loan. The higher you're score, the lower the tier, and the lower the rate.

For instance, a person with a 625 score will pay as much as 3% points more interest than a person with an 800 plus score. Doesn't sound right, but it's the way it is. **The bank is willing to loan the money cheaper to the customer that has the better score,** because they are less of a risk of ever defaulting on the loan. That's what drives the bank.

When the manager on duty pulls your credit score, he is trained to know what lender will best approve your loan with the lowest rate possible. **Why would they want to get you the lowest rate possible?** Because they can **MARK IT UP** as much as two points.

To take advantage of the low payment financing or 0% financing you see on TV or in ads, you have to have a 690 and above credit score. The same thing applies to leasing. They only say in the ads "for well qualified customers". This is what this means. You need a great credit score.

Other things that affect your credit score is excessive shopping. Each time you go to a dealer to buy a car and let them pull your credit, once the deal gets moving along, they will start sending your application to several lenders at once. All dealers us a software system called Dealertrac.com and it does all the work.

It pulls up your credit history, is displays all the lenders that the dealership uses, and once the deal is sent to a lender for approval, it shows the dealer which bank gave the best approval and which one had the best rate and terms.

It updates in real time, and typically **they can have an approval in seconds.** In the old days before the internet, we used have to fax the credit applications over to each back separately and get on the phone with a "buyer" to get approval.

A good finance manager would call his buddy up at ABC bank and argue and plead and rationalize why this deal should be approved. Sometimes he would be successful getting a turndown approved or a better interest rate than originally indicated. It could take hours to get someone approved.

Now it's all done by the time you have gotten up to use the bathroom and returned to the salesperson's desk.

Once the dealership pulls your credit, they won't give you a copy of the total report. But you can ask for a copy of your risk based pricing disclosure. This document will tell you what your credit score is and how it ranks against other consumers.

Dealerships have to provide this for you to sign if you buy a car, but even if you don't buy a car, they must give you a copy if you ask for it.

"Once you get a copy of this, there is no need to let another dealership run your credit."

You know your score now, and it reduces the amount of inquiries on your credit report which can lower your score.

Before you go into the dealership go online and check what your score is. There are many websites that offer to check your credit for free. Also, if you do have credit issues, there are companies available that can "repair" your credit.

They can get certain items deleted off your report which will make your score rise. But it takes several months. So

when you go to the dealership to buy that new or used car,
be prepared by knowing where you stand.

Chapter 9

The Factory Survey, Your Hidden Advantage.

This is referred to as "CSI" or the customer satisfaction index. In today's modern age of automotive new car sales, there is one similarity that ALL manufactures share. The factory survey. Each time a new car is sold, the dealer will report the sale to the factory.

After a couple of days from the time it is reported the factory will send out a survey to the customer asking about their experience. The results that the customer sends back graded and the overall score is attached to the selling dealer.

The factory uses this feedback to determine the overall function of the dealership, how they treat their customers, what experienced the customers are having, and so on. There is a series of around 25 questions on the survey ranging from we're you greeted in a timely fashion? Or, was your car cleaned to your satisfaction?

Was all the paperwork explained in an easy to understand fashion?

Did the salesperson show you how to operate all the features on the car properly? We're you introduced to the service department to schedule your first appointment? And so on. Each question is given a 1 to 10 scoring range.

(1) being the worst to (10) being the best. In the dealership world, a 9 is a bad score. **They want only 10s.**

A dealer that consistently gets mediocre scores comes under a lot of pressure from the factory. The factory can limit the amount of inventory they send the dealership and the factory can put the dealership on a probationary period where everything they do is scrutinized which is no fun for anyone.

And **the most important penalty is to withhold potential money that the dealership gets every quarter for good survey scores.**

Each quarter based on how many new cars they sell the factory sends the dealer a check for each new car sold that quarter as long as the dealer has great "CSI" stores. This can be thousands of dollars.

"And the dealer will go to any means necessary to ensure a perfect "10" survey score from a customer".

Nowadays, the survey comes to the customer via email. The customer simply opens it up, fills out the questions and sends it in. The factory receives it and reports the results to the dealership. The salesperson attached to the survey is alerted to his or her score and they also participate monetarily from the factory for perfect surveys.

135.

Now here is where the catch comes in. If the dealer suspects for any reason that you won't be giving them a perfect survey, they have a problem. They will go to any means necessary to make sure you turn in that "10". They will call you within 3 days of delivery. Not necessarily to make sure you love the car and know how to work everything, **but to make sure you know about the survey coming in your email and "coaching" you on how to fill it out.**

This is highly frowned upon by the factory. One import manufacturer I worked for actually had a question on the survey that asks...

We're you influenced by the dealership to give a favorable score on the survey?

If you answer yes to that question the survey automatically receives a "0"score, and the dealership receives a manipulation or tampering warning.

A few of those a quarter can disqualify the dealer from receiving any quarterly money (which can be around $45,000!) plus the salesperson involved can be reprimanded or even terminated. Bad surveys can cause permanent damage to a dealership.

"Maybe by now you can see the hidden opportunity which is available when the dealer thinks you are not happy".

They will go to extreme methods to make sure that survey either disappears or you become happy. **How do they make it disappear?** They simply put down the wrong email address when they are doing the paperwork.

That way the survey never gets to you. The dealership is not penalized if the survey never gets returned, only if it comes back with a bad score. So NO survey is better that a bad survey.

If during the sales process, like while you are in the finance office or having just left, the salesperson thinks you unhappy for any reason he will tell the manager to "scatter" the survey.

That means to make sure it goes to the wrong email address. Or they make an error by purposely changing one digit or letter in the address and it becomes undeliverable.

It's the same thing. **What you can do to make sure you get your survey** is double check that your correct email address is on all the documents. This is especially true if you are having an unpleasant experience.

You better believe the dealership knows you are not happy, and chances are your email address will be incorrect. If you see it's not correct, demand it be fixed. Sorry but it's just the way it is.

"It's a business based on profits and nothing else".

Now let's say you have dropped the hint that you are not happy. Anything can and will be done to fix your attitude before that survey comes. I have seen customers bring the car back in to be "re cleaned".

I have seen free service coupons given out, I have seen checks cut back to the customer, I have seen free gas fill ups and on and on.

Bottom line, I'm not advocating to slam the dealer on the survey. However, don't let them manipulate you into filling out a false survey just because they told over and over to only give them "10s".

Again this is frowned upon by the factory. If you are unhappy, use it to your advantage, give the dealer a chance to make it up, or get resolution from the dealer, whatever it takes. **Just remember the survey is gold in your pocket and the dealer knows it.** Use it to your advantage whenever you can.

Chapter 10

Understanding Leasing

Most of the material we have covered involved what happens when you purchase a car. Meaning you take out a loan with the intention of paying it off one day and receiving the title.

Or you wrote a check for the entire amount of the car up front and have no outstanding lien or loan on the vehicle. The majority of customers these days still will purchase their cars, but Leasing has made a huge comeback in the last 10 years.

In the early 90s leasing got a bad name because many dealers were doing leases called "open end leases" that required a huge final balloon payment due at the end of the lease that many customers didn't know was coming.

 Today, leasing has been regulated and those leases are no longer used except under certain circumstances. Let's cover the basic understanding of how a lease works.

"First, leasing is basically only agreeing to pay for the first couple of years of the life of the vehicle".

You agree to keep the car for say a 36 month lease, you will drive it, use it, wash and clean it, insure it, everything you would on a traditional purchase EXCEPT at the end of the term be it 24 or 36 months you have 2 options.

1. You can simply turn the car into the dealership and walk away.

2. You can decide to keep the car and finance the remaining balance remaining on the loan, called the "residual value" and keep the car. Now the "residual value" is what the dealership says the car will be worth in 3 years at the start of the lease. When you lease the car, you will walk out and know what your car will be worth in 3 years.

Now very few customers actually take advantage of option 2 and keep the car. Why you may ask? The same reason most customers try to trade every 3 to 4 years, they are tired of the car, their needs have changed in the last 3 years and now they want a SUV or whatever, the car is almost out of the original factory 3 year 36,000 mile bumper to bumper warranty, or they simply saw some latest greatest car on TV and have to have it.

Leasing is a viable option for customers that like to trade every couple of years. **You have no negative equity at the end of the term, the lease is over.**

Sometimes depending on the car and the manufacturers lease rebates and incentives, **the payment can be lower for a 36 month lease than a purchase payment on 72 months.**

A lot of high line manufacturers are having success offering lease deals on their luxury cars and SUVs.

There are some different requirements that need to take place to lease a car. You have to have "perfect credit". The lender that does leasing will require a higher credit score to lease the car over a purchase customer. Also you have to carry higher insurance minimum coverage's over what you would typically need on a purchase.

So your car insurance will be higher when you lease a car over a purchase.

The other major drawback to leasing is the limitation on the miles you are allowed to drive the car during the term of the lease. Most leases these days only allow 12,000 miles per year.

So at end of the 36 month lease you can have no more than 36,000 miles on the car or you pay a penalty of around 15.cents per mile.

Also when you turn the car in after making your last lease payment the dealership stores the car on the back of the lot until the leasing inspector comes out and inspects the car for any damage or scratches or dents or any excessive "wear and tear".

When the excess miles and some dents and dings are added up, **it's not uncommon to see the customer get a**

bill for $2500 to settle up the lease. Most customers that lease understand this and the ones that drive more miles than is offered will lean towards a purchase.

Now, many professional type customers like attorneys or doctor's like to lease simply because of the limited liability it offers them.

What I mean is when you lease the car it is actually registered and titled in the name of the manufacturer with the person that leased the car as a driver or "lessee". This is significant because let's say the doctor is in an accident and it is his fault.

Well if he is leasing the car, the injured parties, attorney can only "go after" or sue the "lessee" which is the manufacturer of the leased car, since they are the primary owner.

The person leasing the car is the "lessor". The doctor's assets or personal finances cannot be touched. This is a great opportunity for professional individuals that have their own practice or business and many do lease only for that reason.

They could care less about the mileage penalty of if the insurance is more, they just don't want to get sued. Many customers are confused about leasing because of the different terminology involved in leasing so let's cover that. We discussed the residual value.

That's what the car will be worth at the end of the lease and what you would have to pay if you wanted to keep the car and finance the balance or "residual amount" remaining.

The residual is important because the larger the residual amount, the lower the payments. Also there is a "money factor". This is the equivalent of an interest rate.

It's the cost to loan you the money. The lower the money factor, the lower the payments also. Capitalization cost or "cap cost" is a confusing term that simply means what you agree to pay for the car.

Most customers get so hung up on the payments of the lease that they forget to make sure they are not paying too much for the car.

When you negotiate a lease, you do the same thing you did on the negotiations of the purchase. You get the best lowest price the dealer will give, you get below his invoice price, you reduce that price by the rebates and lease incentives, and then you ask to have the lease payments figures for 24 or 36 months.

But never longer than that. If you do lease for a longer term you will never be able to get out early, unless you pay a serious penalty.

Why you ask? Because when you lease a car, it is ALMOST impossible to trade it in early before the lease period is up without incurring some serious negative equity. Remember leases are not designed to terminate early.

So the shorter the term, the shorter the time you have the car, and if you get bored or want to do something else, you have a shorter time to be obligated. Now, once you get the payments ask what the money factor is.

This will surprise most managers because the average customer does not know this term. And they should come back with number that looks like this…00034. This is equivalent to around 3 to 4 % in interest.

Just like a traditional loan the dealer can and will mark up the money factor and pocket the proceeds.

You have to know how to ask. Also you want to know what sales price was used to calculate the payment so ask for the "cap cost" price. Again most managers will be shocked you know this term.

You will then get a price and you negotiate just the way you were taught earlier during the purchase portion of the book. Ask for the invoice and reduce the invoice by the dealer "holdback", reduce even further by the rebates and incentives and do not pay the dealer fee.

144.

"Yes, they will still try to charge you the dealer fee even on a lease!"

Once you have done these calculations you should have a good idea of what the payments will be. You can discuss how much the payments are reduced by putting some money down, but typically the more you put down is counterproductive to the reason to lease in the first place.

Why would you want to put a bunch of money down on a car you have to turn back in 36 months later? Remember you don't own the car. Not that the traditional purchase customer that finances his car with a bank owns his car either. Who has the title? The bank does. They own the car.

But that's a matter of opinion. I used to love it when I was presenting a lease and the customer would stand up and beat his chest and proclaim "no way, I own my cars!"

I would say "really Mr. Customer do you have the title? Or does the bank"!

Negotiating a lease with a trade in is no different than a purchase with a trade. **You work one portion at a time.** Get the best lease price, get the best payment and then "sling the trade in". Only settle if you get the researched value for your trade you came in looking for.

Would I recommend leasing over a purchase? It depends on what your personal situation is. What is the car being used for? How many miles do you drive? How often do you trade in your vehicles? Only you can answer these questions. But there are advantages both ways.

This is where you have to be careful. The dealer is very well versed on leasing and when they can't close a customer on a purchase because the payments are a little too high, they will present a lease because the payment is lower, the customer not understanding the lease will jump on it and then remember the old saying "switch and get rich" that's just what the dealer did.

"Typically when a customer is switched to a lease from a traditional retail purchase the profit goes up exponentially".

Leases usually have more gross profit only because today's customers don't know how to negotiate the lease or understand it. If you are trading in a vehicle that is a purchase and has some negative equity, leasing your next car is away to "stop the cycle" of rolling the negative equity into the next loan and so on.

"Because once the lease is up you're done. No more payments are due and you can simply walk away".

Beware of advertisements that offer to terminate your lease early and put you into another lease or purchase while you still have payments remaining. This is called a "lease pull a head program".

146.

If you do that, the lease lender or **bank will charge you a "disposition fee" or early termination fee which can be as much as $895 depending on the lending institution.**

The dealer will not tell you about this penalty, and you will get a bill for it about a month after you traded in your lease. You have to know about this penalty and get the dealer to agree to pay it. He will, but only if you know to ask.

Hopefully by now, **you have learned many "inside industry secrets"** like the one I just gave you. Any one of these will more than cover the cost of this book.

"If you read this book and only use a couple of the many strategies I have given you, thousands of dollars will be saved on your next purchase".

Remember, knowledge is definitely power when you are dealing with car dealerships. Take a minute and contemplate that word. "Dealerships" where did it come from?

The word "dealer" means "to barter or negotiate" and that is the essence of what the car business is.

"Everything in negotiable".

You just have to know what to negotiate and how to ask for it. Customers will always want to "haggle" when they buy or lease a car. Dealers tried the "no haggle" "one price" selling systems.

Remember the Saturn franchise? It sold some nice American made cars that were affordable and cutting edge. The prices were all set up front, no negotiations needed or allowed, and for a while they sold like crazy. But eventually the numbers dwindled because buyers still want to feel like they "got a deal".

They want to go home and say "I really stuck it to that new car dealer on the deal I got on my car". Little do they know the dealer made $4000 off the front and back of the deal and "stole" his trade and will clean it up and make another $2000 when he sells that!

I recently saw a survey that put the car buying experience right up there with "visiting the mother in law" or "having a root canal" or even "getting an IRS audit".

The people that have these experiences are the ones that are ill prepared. You are not this buyer. You have been educated, you have a strategy, you will do your research and not buy on impulse or emotion, and be willing to "walk away". **One of the biggest questions I get the most often is,**

"Jackson, when do I know I have the best deal?"

This is how you know. When you stand up and start walking out and the dealer let's you leave, that's when you know, because that means he is done, he can't go any lower. I have had customer's do this and I said "let them leave" and they went out to their car and came back in and said "wrap it up, we will take it".

Why? Because they knew I was all in. They had reached the bottom of the barrel. I was not willing to lose anymore. And sometimes this happens, **but if you use my strategy, and are at the dealership at the right time and on the right car, magic can happen.**

Remember, customers buy cars from dealer's everyday in this country, and dealers sometimes lose money on these deals, but the next customer that rolls in "lays down" and "boom" all the money the dealer lost on the last deal is forgotten because he just made $6000 on this deal. That's how it works. **Eventually the house always wins.**

Chapter 11

Purchasing a Pre-Owned Car

Buying a used car can sometimes be advantageous for several reasons. First, a pre owned car or "used car" typically has already taken the depreciation hit that new cars take when you drive them off the lot.

Another words, say you just bought a 2015 Nissan Altima S. This is the base model. You negotiated and bought the car UNDER invoice and received rebates and incentive and refused to pay the dealer fee.

If one month later, you took that car back to the dealer you would be devastated to learn what they would give you in trade. Normally, even if it only had 40 miles on it, the car is technically "used" because it has been titled to someone therefore it can never be sold as a new car again.

The used car manager will look the car over for damage etc...and then go to the new car manager and ask what true dealer cost was on this car a month ago.

Let's just say it cost the dealer after "holdback" and all hidden discounts and dealer cash from the factory, $20,000. The used car manager would then reduce that price by 25%. So that car is now worth around $15,000 with only 40 miles on it and only being 1 month old!

Ouch. So if you went online and found a used 2015 Nissan Altima S and even if it had 15,000 miles on it, you could probably find one for around that price of $15,000. Dealers go to auctions every week and buy these cars from rental companies and place them on their lot for "switch cars". Remember? "switch and get _____" That's correct rich.

You come on the lot and negotiate a really low price on a new one, and they tell you they can get to your price on the same car only it is used with some miles on it. It's the same year and has the same equipment.

But now they are going to make some serious money off you because you can't believe it's that much cheaper.

So buying a used car can be a smart and affordable alternative. There are many ways to get the values of used cars.

Many websites like Autotrader.com or Cars.com advertise used cars from all over the country, you simply log on and put in your zip code and start comparing prices. If you find one at your local dealer, BEFORE you show up, you must be prepared.

"Some dealers make more money off their used cars than their new cars."

How is that you ask? Well first off, used cars are not as easy to compare price wise, because there is not many of the same identically equipped used cars in your area. Or the dealer may have the only one around and he knows this. Remember the dealer software appraisal system we discussed?

Well this also tells him how many of the used cars like his are in the area and what they are selling for, so he knows how to price them.

Also every day, websites like Autotrader.com and Cars.com which are paid by the dealers to list their cars, run a computer update and download the dealers used cars and prices.

Dealers have learned that used cars that are online, get sold faster if they have pictures attached or even walk around videos.

Companies come out and do this for the dealer for a fee. I would say that **the majority of used cars sold today off new car dealers lots are from the internet.** Dealers can list all the used cars they have, and reach a much broader audience.

But even with all this technology at their finger tips, **you can still "beat the dealer" and get an amazing deal or even get the dealer to lose money on a used car.** Here is how to do it.

You must be prepared. Just like on the new car you must do your research, you may call the dealership and get some information over the phone. (More about internet and phone sales later) You need to get the Carfax and make sure the car has had no accidents.

You need to get an idea of the value. I was in a large "big box" bookstore the other day and right on the shelf in the automotive section was the Kelly Blue Book. These types of books have all the pricing on all makes and models and you can even go on KBB.com which is their website and get pricing. NADA also produces a yellow book that has all the used car values.

So assuming you have done all that, print all the pricing quotes you can and go to the dealership and check out the car. As I said you want to make sure the car hasn't been wrecked, how are the tires, has the car been smoked in?

Look around the edges of the windows to see if any "overspray" is found. **Remember sometimes cars are wrecked and painted and the Carfax never picks it up**.

Drive the car, how much of the factory warranty is available? What are the miles, taking into consideration normal miles are 12,000 miles per year. Anymore than that constitutes a deduction in value in the book.

Assuming the car checks out and you can live with it, go inside and prepare to "do battle".

Again, the salesperson will do his thing filling out the CRM information on his computer, and even though he noticed the nicely shined up car you drove up in, **refrain from discussing the possibility of trading a car.** All you want to do at this point is isolate the price of the used car you want to buy.

A good well trained dealership will send the salesperson back with the "list" price of the car with a +++ sign underneath the price. This +++ sign is simply plus tax, tag, and title, (and the dealer fee) which you are not going to pay. Then it will show a range of payment options with different down payment amounts. Remember that? With $2000 down, payments would be $320s-$360s W.A.C. What's the WAC? With approved credit.

This is the way car dealers want to work car deals if you let them. The least information possible (less for you to object to) and close you strictly on payments with the logic, well Mr. Customer, the monthly payments are what you are really paying for the car correct?

"So if we get the payments where you want, obviously all the other numbers must be in line."

This is called the "payment close". And once you tell the salesperson you are interested or willing to finance at the dealership you just became a "payment buyer."

The dealership knows that by doing this you really don't know a lot of important numbers that went into figuring that payment.

You don't know the term of the loan, the longer they stretch out your term, the more you pay for the car. A 72 month payment of $300 is a lot more than a 60 month payment of $300 right?

Also by now the salesperson has a good idea of what your credit situation is and they used a generic interest rate of say 6% to figure your payments. Also, they have the dealer fee figured into the total amount you are financing or the "out the door price". And don't forget the "list price" they casually wrote or printed out.

That's the equivalent of the full "list price" with the "addendum" or the dealer "add on" sticker on new cars. But hold up, you are prepared and tell the salesperson or manager if he has already come over to "cool his jets".

You want to separate out what are you really paying for the car. So simply tell them all you want to know is what is the best price on the car? Now as we said earlier, most new car dealers sell their used car on the internet. They have the online price and this price is reduced each week depending on how old it is and how close it is to the dealership's "turn policy", remember that?

That's the day when the car has to leave the lot, one way or another. Even though the car is on the internet for say $13,997, they will assume you don't know that, and quote you a price of $15,997.

I have seen dealers that get customers to agree to the higher price, and then go online (while the customer is sitting in the dealership) and change the online price from $13,997 to $15,997 just in case you happen to go online on your phone and research the car.

"This only happens to the buyer that is not prepared, but came in on an impulse to buy a car."

Pretty slick huh? By now you should be reading this book and really "shaking your head." You are probably saying **"I had no idea these dealerships were so sophisticated and clever."** Well wake up! Every day they are training and planning for your visit, practicing and role playing every possible scenario, **to separate you from your money.** Just like the casino.

This is their business. They are hoping and praying that you are not prepared, you are uniformed, you have not done your research, you are going along with their "road to a sale" **and at the end of the road is a "pot of gold" and guess who get's it? The dealer.**

"But you are not that customer, because you invested in this book and you are prepared".

And **if you use my proven strategy, it will work and you will save thousands.** Yes I said "thousands".

So back to the main objective when purchasing a used car, isolate the selling price from all the other confusing options placed in front of you. You know the online price, you have researched what a fair price for the car is and you simply make a "counteroffer".

You may say **"I see you have the list price of the car here for $15,997 but I went online last night and saw the car listed for $13,997? What happened to that price? I was prepared to offer you the $13,997 for the car but after looking at the car in person and driving it....**

I noticed the tires are looking worn and the a/c didn't blow as cold as it should, so I'm prepared to offer you 13,000 plus tax, tag, and title, and I'm not paying the dealer fee."

I put that entire paragraph in bold because you should memorize it and practice it over and over so it rolls off your tongue. You just did to the dealer what he does to customers every day. You **DEVALUED** his car!

Remember when the salesperson silently went around your trade in and put his finger on all he scratches and dings and dents and felt the tire wear depth?

That's what you do to the used car you are trying to buy. Now obviously, this won't work on new car purchases because they are perfect.

But on a used car, the more things you can find wrong with the car, you can use to your advantage to either get the price reduced, or have them fixed for no extra charge. Now the salesperson has a problem.

He has to go back to the desk and tell his manager that you saw the car online for $13,997 and your counter offer is only $13,000 because of the couple of issues you found with the car.

The first thing the manager will do is look to see how long he has had the car.

Then he will come back with the "split the difference close" and say "I will sell you the car for the online price (he has to, it's advertised, "gee thanks") but I cannot reduce the price for any reason because if it's online for that price, it wouldn't be fair to everyone else if I sold it to you for cheaper."

Are you kidding me? Don't believe it. **They do it every day.**

"The best price is the price you agree to and they are willing to take!"

160.

At this point what do you do? What have you been taught to do in this book? That's correct. You stand up, (the receptionist that is strategically placed in the showroom will alert the desk that you are up) and kindly thank the salesperson for their time, ask for a card, (they hate that because they know you are not buying today) and slowly start heading for the door.

If they are willing to sell you a car for a lower price they will stop you, and they always do. The manager will run over and say "Mr. Customer, hold on, where do we have to be to make this deal happen? Now you got them. You say "I made you an offer and you declined, so no problem I will keep shopping."

He will sit you back down and try to split the difference between the online price of $13,900 and your offer of $12,900 so "how about $13,500 +++?" At that point you can bring up the things on the car that bothered you and either take the deal or "split the difference again to re-offer $12,250 +++.

"Why do I keep using the term "split the difference"?

Because psychologically it plays on your sense of "fair play" it suggest that if I (the manager) am willing to come up some, you should be willing to come down some, and **hopefully we can "meet in the middle" and we both win.**

If I say Mr. Customer, we are $2000 away from where I am and your offer, I tell you what, If I come down a thousand dollars and you come up a thousand dollars can we in "fairness" meet in the middle for $1000?

That sounds fair doesn't it? Everyone gets something. The dealer feels like he raised you $1000, and you feel like you lowered him $1000.

It's a win/win. And it works. When you leave the dealership you want to feel as if you "showed the dealer up" and got the deal you wanted. The dealer wants to get rid of a car that is old or slow moving or simply just sell a car to get the day going.

The problem is most if not all the customers today have no idea (because they haven't read this book) that what they thought was a "good deal" was in fact a "great deal" for the dealer.

"They are looking out the window for you to drive away so then everyone can celebrate!"

I'm telling you it happens every day in dealerships all over this country. So let's continue with this deal on the used car. You **finally** got the selling price you wanted for the used car, and now you just simply follow the steps we already covered when purchasing a new car, with a few exceptions.

There will be NO rebates or incentives like on the new car. That only comes from the factory, and doesn't apply to used cars. There is no "invoice" on a used car.

You have isolated the best price on the used car. You then casually ask the salesperson "say, what would my trade be worth" (this is our strategy called "slinging in the trade") and you refer to what we have already covered on getting the most for your trade in the trade-in chapter.

If you have no trade you then want to see a print out of all the figures and they will produce a buyers order with the "out the door price". Look this document over and….

"Make sure you are not being charged the Dealer fee"

Believe me when I say they will "slip it in". Remember? Most dealers have it hard printed on the buyers order anyway, you will have to cross through it and say **"I'm not paying the dealer fee."**

This may involve another visit from the manager but hold your ground, they will remove the charge, but you have to be firm.

They will try to say "this fee covers the cost to process your paperwork" or "it covers the salaries of the girls in accounting" whatever, don't fall for it, its pure profit.

Ok, so you got a great price and refused to pay the dealer fee, great job! Now you are ready to decide how you want to pay for the car. Hopefully, by reading this book you have done your homework and know your finance options.

From here on out, follow the steps we covered on using the dealership financing. Just because it is a used car, don't be fooled into thinking anything is different when it comes to financing.

Remember, they just probably lost money on the used car you agreed to buy, they hope to make it up on the financing and products sold by the finance manager.

Now there are a couple of caveats or slight variations on financing a used car verses a new car. First off, sometimes depending on how old the car is the interest rate will be higher on the used car. That's normal.

Banks simply charge a higher "buy rate" to the dealer on a used car regardless of your credit. Let's say you are buying a 1 year old Nissan with 12,000 miles on it. The rate will be around 1% to 1.5% higher than the new car interest rate.

Also the term will be shorter on a used car than a new car. Not by much, but you can't expect to get 72 months financing on a 6 year old car. If you do, the interest rate will be a lot higher than it should be and counterproductive.

When you get into the finance office, all the same extra products will be attempted to be sold to you, only they become more expensive. Take for instance the extended warranty.

The warranty company (owned by the dealer) will charge different amounts based on the age and miles of the car. Import used cars extended warranties typically are more expensive and the higher the miles the higher the price.

You have to determine if the car you are buying has any factory warranty remaining, remember most new cars today have 2 warranties that come free of charge and are transferrable.

So you can assume the warranty remaining, if the 3 year 36,000 bumper to bumper warranty is not remaining then maybe the 5 year 60,000 mile power train warranty is. Great, you fill out some paperwork and send it in and you have a warranty on the car that didn't cost you a dime.

But let's assume there is no warranty available. All dealers in America are by law required to get you to sign a Federal As-Is document. This document states that either the car has a warranty, or the car has NO warranty.

Dealers are required to display this document in the window of the used car where the new car window sticker would go. Most of the time the box that says" No Warranty" will be checked.

That does not mean you cannot buy an extended warranty on the car. It just means that as of now, no warranty remains.

This document is important because you have to sign the back of it, it goes into your stack of paperwork and the dealer will use it against you if you don't buy a warranty and have a problem later.

"Most customers are under the delusion, that they have a period of time that covers the repairs on a car of say 30 days."

When they return to the dealership to complain that the a/c stopped working a week after they bought the car, the manager will pull out the "As-Is" form you signed and show it to you. It says in black and white "that no warranty exists on this vehicle whether implied by the dealership employee verbally or in writing" **legally, you are beat.**

That document is "bullet proof." I have been summoned to court before because a customer was suing the dealership for repairs. The judge would listen to the customer rattle off all the things wrong with the car, and the costs of all the repairs needed, and let them go on and on.

Then when they had "vented" everything that they are unhappy about, the judge would turn to me and simply ask one question.

"Mr. Dealer? Do you have the signed AS-IS document?"

Yes sir your honor, its right here. The judge will look it over and ask the customer if this is their signature on the back. They will start explaining about all the repairs, or they didn't know what they were signing (that's because remember all the documents the finance manager slid in front of them) blah, blah, blah and **the judge will say "Dismissed".**

I've seen it happen over 20 times in my career. **I have never lost** and had to fix the repairs, if I had the signed "As-Is" document in my possession.

This brings up a good point. Most dealers will have no problem with you taking the used car you are interested in to an outside mechanic to have the car inspected.

Most mechanics will find something wrong the car, (because they want to make some money) and will give you a print out with the repairs needed, and you can present this to the manager when you are negotiating the price. Most dealers will listen.

But let's return to the warranty. I know I said that "I would not recommend buying the extended warranty on the new car." **But on the used car, sometimes it can be advantageous.** Keep in mind that the price the dealer charges you is always a lot higher than a price you can get from an outside source.

There are many companies on the internet that offer extended warranties on used cars. Your insurance agent most instances sells warranties on used and new cars. I recently bought my teenage daughter her first car (a used one) from a dealer.

I did not buy the warranty they offered. About a week later I received about 4 solicitations in the mail offering to sell me a warranty on the car I bought. I called one of them and the price was very reasonable. It was about a $1000 cheaper than the one offered by the dealer.

"You can imagine what it's like when I go into a dealership to buy a car".

I have been paid by customers to go in to the dealership and help them negotiate the deal. I have saved these customers thousands of dollars. The dealerships don't know who I am, but they are glad when I leave. (This service is available to you as well).

It's like a professional "card counting" blackjack gambler walking into a casino and taking all their money. They hate it. Most casinos will take the guys picture and put it in a book and send it to all the other casinos and tell them to be on the lookout for this "advantage player".

"When you finish this book, you will be an "advantage player".

That's all you can ask for. You want to walk in knowing all the obstacles that are in front of you designed to "separate you from your money" just like a casino. A reason to possible purchase the warranty from the dealer is you won't have to come out of pocket later for the lump sum.

What I mean is say the warranty is $1800. You can include it with your loan, which is like an extra $30 per month. That sounds a lot better than having to scratch a check off for this amount later because you decide to buy a warranty.

Also, **most dealership warranties on used cars don't become valid until you have had the car at least 30 days.** Some are 90 days!

Why is that you ask? Because remember, the Dealer owns the warranty company, and he doesn't want to have to take money out of his warranty company to cover repairs that the car has if he doesn't have to.

My experience has been that if you do buy the warranty on a used car, and have problems soon after you bought the car, **the dealer will cover the repairs if you cause enough trouble.**

The used car warranty will have a minimum deductible around $100 per repair per incident. That means each time you come in you pay that $100 first. Don't forget **the dealer also owns the service department and can control what he pays for labor and parts.**

"A lot of time the deductible you just paid will more than cover the repairs to your car!"

And the dealer still has your $1800 in his warranty account that is in an off shore bank drawing ridiculous returns. I know dealers that make so much money over the years just off their warranty company, that when they retire, **they have millions in that account.** It's a huge profit center. So be educated and aware, do your homework, and you will be fine.

"What if you wanted to buy a used car from a private party seller?

What are the Pro's and Con's of that? The main advantage is depending on what state you live in, you don't **have to pay any sales tax.**

For instance, Georgia does not charge you sales tax when you register a used car you purchased from a private seller. This can be huge. On a $10,000 car it's around $700 in savings.

Also, you can get a better understanding of the history of the car because you are dealing with the person that has been driving the car sometimes since it was new.

They will have all the service records or you can copy the VIN number and for a fee of around $35 run a Carfax yourself and see what has been done to the car, if it has been in any accidents, if it has a salvage or rebuilt title. **A salvage or rebuilt title is important to know.**

This means that at some previous time the car was in a serious accident and the insurance deemed the car a "total loss". The insurance company then pays the owner for the wrecked car, and then they take it to an "insurance auction" that sells the car to junk yards or salvage yards or parts companies.

These places will sometimes "fix the wrecked cars" by putting all new front "clips" or rear ends on the car and sell them to used car dealers. **New car dealer won't sell salvage cars.** Most states require that you take the car to a special inspector to make sure the car is safe.

It's a hassle, and **the car is worth half its true value if it has a salvage title.** You can find out by asking the owner if he has the title with him. If he does it will say on the title if it is salvaged or rebuilt. You have to look closely.

In Florida, it shows up real small in a tiny box towards the top of the title. You can buy a rebuilt car from someone and if you are not careful you will never know it. When you to register the car, they will tell you. And then it's too late.

If the dealer takes in a trade that is a salvage or rebuilt car, it goes straight to the auction and the auctioneer has to announce over the intercom to all the bidders that this vehicle has a salvage or rebuilt title.

Most used car dealers will simply walk away. Nobody wants the aggravation or liability associated with selling this car.

So let's assume the car you are looking at has a clean title and also no liens recorded on it. Private sellers can borrow money sometimes on a car and when they do, a lien is recorded with the state by the person that loaned the money, like a title pawn place.

These places have become very popular lately. When you look at the title, you have to be careful to see if a lien is recorded. If it is don't buy the car.

You won't be able to register it without satisfying or paying off that lien. Sometimes it can be thousands of dollars.

Another trick some private sellers will pull off is to take their title to a place and borrow money on it. Well it takes around a week to record the lien once the company sends the information into the DMV.

The seller will run down to the DMV the day before they take out the loan and say they "lost their title and need a duplicate title printed out."

So they have two titles, one they give the lending institution that will get a lien put on it, and the one they just got from the DMV that has no lien recorded.

I have had this happen to me on trades from crooked customers at the dealership. We don't catch it until weeks later. A lot of times the customer is long gone. You however, are unaware and this can be devastating.

Look for amazing low prices on a nice car. **If it's too good to be true, it usually is.** Also be leery if the seller is willing to drop the price ridiculous amounts. This can also be a red flag. None of these things happen at a licensed dealership.

A popular website that a lot of people buy and sell cars is Craigslist. You have to really be careful. There are a lot crooked people that sell cars on Craigslist. One of the biggest problems are the people that list their car for sale under the "by owners" section.

"A lot of times these people who are representing themselves as the owner of the car are not legally the true owner."

What do I mean? How could they have the title and not be the real owner? Here's what they do. They search Craigslist everyday and go look at cars for sale by owners.

They will buy the car from the true registered owner, and instead of registering it in their name which is what they are legally required to do, **they simply clean the car up a little, fix some minor things that are wrong, take some better glossy pictures and repost the car on Craigslist for a $1000 profit or more!**

This is called "title jumping" or selling a car "open title". It's also illegal. You are not dealing with the true registered owner of the car.

You don't know if the car is stolen, or if this person really has permission to sell the car or have any recourse if there is a problem registering it because this person is long gone! The only way you can be sure that this is not the case, is to ask the person selling the car if you can see their license and then compare it to the name on the title.

Usually these sellers will agree to meet you in a public place like a mall parking lot. They won't be selling it from their house. Normally true private sellers will have you come to their house and the pictures taken of the car that is for sale, will be in their driveway, or in front of their house.

The other guy will take pictures of the car in a parking lot, or behind some building. You really have to be careful.

Also, bring someone with you when you are looking at a car on Craigslist or some over website. Remember this person knows you are coming to see the car and may have cash; this could set you up for a potentially bad situation.

If you do agree to buy the car, and the cash amount is substantial, agree to do the transaction at your bank. They will gladly let you use their facility to handle your business.

You also want to get a signed bill of sale; many states like Florida require it along with the title to register the car. The bank can print you one. Again, **"buyer beware" when you are dealing with the public.**

But what about buying a used car from a small licensed independent used car dealer? Well, most are licensed and bonded with the state that they operate in. And for the most part are reputable. But, you need to know where they get their used cars from.

Most get them from the auction. The small independent dealers flock there to buy all the "new car trades" the big new car dealers don't want to mess with. These cars either have too many miles, or bad Carfax's, or salvage titles, or are just too old.

The cars will be shined up and cleaned by the new car dealer and delivered to the auction. The cars will run one after the other until they are all sold.

Most of the time, as long as the cars bring "close" to what the dealer has in them, they will sell. Dealers will sometimes lose money on a car at the auction just to be done with it.

These small used car dealers buy these cars under what is called a "red light". That means that the cars are sold As-is. Once the sale is final the used car dealer owns it. If he goes out 10 minutes later to start the car and it won't run, too bad he bought it.

 The auctions cater to the big new car dealers because they bring so many cars to the auction each week to sell. **The auction is the one that really makes out because they get a fee from the seller and the buyer.** Why is all this important?

"Because if there is a nice shiny used car on the independent used car dealer's lot, you have to wonder why the new car dealer didn't keep it himself and try to sell it."

These cars usually have issues and the new car dealer doesn't want to deal with the aggravation or the "heat" if the customer has problems with the car later or even worse if the customer gets in an accident due to some issue mechanically with the car. Then he can get sued. And no new car dealer wants to deal with that.

The independent used car dealer usually will use some "cheap shade tree" mechanic that lives behind his building to fix or "bandage" up the cars he has bought at the auction, using parts from junk yards and other cars. Not all small used car dealers do this, but a large majority do.

They also have to charge sales tax just like the new car dealer, but their process is not nearly as complicated as the new car dealer. They generally deal in cash, some offer some financing, but it's typically tailored for people with credit issues so the interest rates are enormous.

Many small used car dealers operate what is called "buy here pay here" lots. This simply means the dealer himself is the bank. He is loaning you the money and charging the state maximum interest rate.

Also, once he realizes you don't have cash and need his financing, his price for the car jumps up like $3000. "**Oh, that's my financing price the cash price is much lower.**" This buyer will be required to bring in payments by the week, not the month.

This is so if you miss a payment, you don't get too far away with only a week head start, instead of a month to realize you are not paying for the car.

They will repossess the car after one missed payment. They then get to keep the car and all the money you paid, and after holding it for 30 days, resell the car to someone else. I know of used car lots like these that have millions of dollars "on the books".

Then they sell the accounts to a business collection company for around 60 cents on the dollar, get a huge check and are done. They don't have to collect anymore payments, or go looking for non paying customers. It's the problem of the new company that purchased the accounts.

The good news if the customer does not make the payments on time, or has a car repossessed, it won't affect their credit because **these places don't report to the credit bureaus.** When these customers come into the new car dealership and try to trade in their "buy here pay here" car, it's really sad how upside down they are. It's not uncommon to see someone owe $12,000 on a $4000 car.

The only thing left that is important to cover involving used cars is the all popular "CPO" or "certified pre-owned" deals you see on TV. These are only offered by new car dealers and they are getting popular. A "CPO" car is simply a 1 to 3 year old trade in, or a car they bought at the auction that is a lease turn in, meaning the lease was up and the customer turned it in. The new car dealer will then put it thru an inspection process, put a clean Carfax sticker on the windshield and try to sell it as a super clean used car. Most times it is.

The biggest advantage to buying one of these cars is they come with a 7 year 100,000 limited warranty along with whatever factory warranty is left on the vehicle to start with. You just have to do your homework on the pricing and value of these cars BEFORE you arrive at the dealership to know their true value.

These are typically great "switch and get ___ "rich" cars, ("just checking to see if you are paying attention"). If they can't get to your numbers on a new car, they will attempt to show you the "CPO" cars. Some dealers sell several every month. My experience is that they are hard to sell. But you must decide that for yourself.

What about buying a new car "Demo" or demonstration car? These have been around for years but in today's world not many dealer's let employees have demos anymore.

A demo is simply when the employee is allowed to take a new car and drive it as a perk for working at the dealership. When I first got in the car business in the late 80s, everyone got a demo. It was one of the best reasons to work there! All the salesman and managers got one, and other managers in the dealership also got one.

But over time after salespeople began going out and getting DUIs, dealer's started paying ridiculous amounts in insurance. So the demos were taken away from everyone but the most important managers.

I once worked at a large dealership where the service manager, was drinking and driving in his demo, ran a red light, hit a lady and put her through the windshield. She had to have reconstructive surgery and the next day, I had to turn in my demo along with everyone else that worked there.

"The biggest thing to understand about the demo is it will have up to 7000 miles on it."

This is important because these miles get subtracted from the factory warranty miles allowed on the car. So as soon as you drive it home, 7000 miles have already been reduced from the miles you have remaining on the warranty coverage. Dealers understand this and will offer you special deals and incentives on these cars.

They are technically still considered "new cars" because they have never been titled or registered to anyone. So you still get all the rebates and factory incentives that come with buying a new car.

180.

However you need to make sure the discount in price justifies the miles off the warranty. Usually these cars are always "aged" or old which is another reason to get a great price.

"My strategy would be to offer the dealer a couple of thousand under the "invoice amount" minus all rebates and incentives, and minus the dealer "holdback, and don't pay the dealer fee!"

Hopefully, you have a better understanding of the inner workings of the used car world, and are better prepared to purchase a used car whether it's from a new car dealer, a used car dealer or a private seller. Good luck.

Chapter 12

Pressure Tactics by the Dealer

Remember when I said the salesperson is programmed to try and get you to buy the car today? Well everything that is done at a dealership is designed to make this happen. Because they know that less than 10% of all customers that leave ever come back.

And it's true. Sure the customer will promise to come back even making an appointment for a certain time the next day but they rarely do.

"That's why the mantra in the car business that is taught "over and over again" is "buyers are liars."

That right, dealerships don't trust customers because they will make them bend over backwards and then go buy the same car across town for $100 less money. It's true.

I guess customers think the dealers are so dishonest anyway that customer's that would never lie or mislead anyone, will do so to a car salesperson. They feel it's justified.

And it's a shame, but I have personally witnessed customers do dishonest and shameful things and over time if you are in the car business, you get "callused" to the feelings of customers. It's just the way it is. But because customer's have promised to do this or do that so many times and not delivered the ....

"Dealerships have had to resort to "pressure tactics" to sell cars".

It's just so competitive because manufacturers will stack the same franchise 30 miles apart from each other and let them "fight it out". I've worked in dealerships where the nearest (same manufacturer dealership) was 15 miles away! So you can see their need for urgency.

They hold sales meetings every day teaching "there is no tomorrow" today is all we have!

So when you get to the dealership their attitude towards you is **"they have to do everything in their power to get you to "sign on the line that is dotted" today."**

Here are some pressure tactics.

If you show up without the other "decision maker" they will offer to get them on the phone, or better yet, "let's drive over and pick them up!"

If you don't have your checkbook for the down payment with you, they will tell you don't worry you can bring the check back later (as long as you drive the car off the lot).

If you don't have your trade- in with you they will offer to appraise your car "sight unseen" and put a value on your trade based on what you say the condition is.

If you bring the car in and it's not in the condition you say, they will try to reduce the trade allowance (which never works, but they try).

If you don't have the draft from the credit union or bank that you are using to buy the car with, they will say "it's not a problem you can bring it in later".

If you are using a co-signer and the co-signer lives out of state and is not with you, they will "overnight the paperwork to them".

If the car you want is not on the lot because of color or options they will "dealer trade" to get it. That's when they go into the factory computer and see which dealer is the closest to their location and has the car, and trade them whatever car they want for it.

If you simply want to "sleep on the deal" and go home, remember they will try to get you take the car or be "de-horsed". So that way they know you will have to come back.

If you can't quite decide on the figures, they will offer to have you sign all the paperwork, take the car and they will "hold the paperwork at the managers desk" for 24 hours, and if you change your mind, bring the car back.

If you don't have car insurance, they will get you on the phone with an agent, or go online and add the car to your policy.

If you are buying the car for someone else and want to wait till they are in town or coming home to deliver the car, they will offer to store the car on the back of the lot, and deliver it when you are ready.

If you don't have your proof of income that the bank sometimes requires, they will offer to go online and get you to print out your bank statements showing your deposits of your paychecks.

If the bank requires a co-signer, and you don't have one, they will offer to call and go pick up the person that agrees to co-sign.

If the car you are trading in does not run, they will offer to get it towed to the dealership.

If you don't know the exact payoff amount on your trade, they have the numbers to all the banks, and will call and do this for you.

If you are getting your money from an IRA or from Investments and it takes some time to get the money,

they will take a personal check from you and hold it till you have transferred the funds.

If you don't have the required down payment the bank requires in some instances, they will hold a check until it is good. Sometimes as long as 30 days!

If the person who is going on the loan with you is not present and credit cannot be pulled, they will offer to call the person and get them to fill out a credit application online so it is legal to pull it or "check it".

If you are registering the car out of state, they will mail the paperwork to the out of state DMV for you so you can take the car that day.

Maybe by now, you are getting the picture. **Yes the dealer does pressure you.**

"They want to anticipate any scenario that would involve you leaving without the car."

Because they know that if you leave without the car, they have nothing. No way to get you back in. And all that time and effort was for nothing. Nobody gets paid.

"At the very minimum a good manager will get 30% of customers who want to leave to take the car home overnight."

This is a powerful pressure tactic. Because they know once you get it home and the neighbors see it and come over and compliment you on the "shiny new car" or your kids get see it and freak out with joy, you my friend, are "done".

How else do you explain to everyone what happened to the new car? They may think your credit was bad and the bank wouldn't approve you, or you simply couldn't afford it, or who knows what.

But once you drive that car away, **the dealership knows that you will at least be returning.** It's guaranteed. 100%.

You have to come back either way, if you are coming back to tell them you don't want the car, they get another chance to "sweeten the deal" or put you in a car that will work or whatever they have to do…but **they don't get that chance if you leave in your own car**, and they can only hope you will return.

It's a long wait. Believe me, I've been there.

"That's why they have to do everything possible to get you to buy while you are there".

Customers understand this, I have gone over to introduce myself to a potential customer and the first thing out of their mouth is "we are not buying today" or "we are just looking, not doing anything today" and I just rolled over it. Salespeople hear this every day.

It's just a smoke screen they think. Salespeople are trained today that "the word no" is just a request for more information, and you should get 5 "no's" before you close a sale.

You have to be steadfast in your ability to walk away from the wrong deal. No matter what they say or what time of the month it is, **that deal will be there tomorrow**.

The only circumstance I can think of when the deal could change in one day is when you come in on the last day of the month, and the next day is the start of a new month, and **sometimes the rebates add incentives can change.**

If you're not a confrontational person, **bring someone with you** that is, we call that person the "car lawyer" or "third base coach". He is the guy doing all the negotiating and has nothing to do with paying for the car.

A good manager can tear him apart. I can personally say the dealerships motto is **"our job is to talk someone into doing something they don't want to do"** and it's done every day.

Chapter 13

The Internet Age and What It's Done to Selling Cars

There is no doubt the internet has changed the car business. Dealers are heavily invested in "digital advertising" and "digital media". They understand the importance of reaching a broad audience, and getting their message out as quickly and inexpensively as possible. There are tons of seminars teaching dealerships how to successfully utilize the internet.

Dealers now have rooms filled with work stations staffed by employees that do nothing but handle internet leads, respond to emails or live chats, and send text messages. Dealers today can send out a 10,000 email blast in minutes that costs them nothing.

They spend money on ad words and with "Google" to make sure that their dealership comes up first in search engines when you put in a search. Dealers employ what is called a "BDC" which stands for a "business development department".

When you see a car on Autotrader.com that belongs to a new car dealer, a message is sent to the dealer giving him your information, like your email address or contact information etc. These people only get paid when a customer "shows" or when you set an appointment and

you show up. Dealerships train these individuals on how
to answer the sales calls coming in with a script that is
"taped to their desks".

The only purpose in life for these people is not to sell you a
car. **It is to set the appointment and make sure you show
up.** They will tell you that you are a "VIP" customer and
when you arrive, they will have the car you want pulled
out front and ready for your inspection.

The lead is passed on to the managers, who may call you
to confirm the appointment, and then give it to a
salesperson to get the car ready.

I'm not necessarily advocating that there is anything
wrong with this however, just as long as you remember
everything involves getting you into the dealership. They
will tell you anything you want to hear over the phone to
get you in.

You may ask them, is the car on the lot? They will say
"sure it is" Mr. Customer. Do you have it in blue? Sure we
do Mr. Customer.

Can I get the 0% financing? Yes you can Mr. Customer. It
doesn't matter what special incentive you are inquiring
about, because they know **whatever dealership you
physically visit, chances are that's where you will buy a
car and their job it to get you to visit them!**

I have worked many direct mail sales, remember those? We discussed them in the advertising chapter? These are the mailers that come directly to your mailbox with your name and trade specifically tailored to you. Many are misleading and reduced to trickery to get you come in. One in particular I remember had a scratch off lottery ticket attached to the outside of it.

Once you scratched it off, it looked like you won $2000. It really did. All you have to do is come in and claim your winnings **you didn't have to buy a car**. The phones were ringing off the hook. Our BDC people were telling people "absolutely, you are a winner! When can you be here".

People that didn't have a car were taking buses to get to the dealership, people that had no job were coming to the dealership, people came in on bicycles it was ridiculous.

They didn't want to talk about a car, or drive a car or do anything but claim that money. Nobody won the $2000. And a lot of people left upset. The managers have to put out all the "heat". It was a nightmare. But if you look in your mailbox, I bet you get one of these mailers all the time.

"Again, it's not the message that matters all they want to do is get you in the door".

All internet traffic is designed to do is flood the doors with people.

All dealerships have sophisticated websites, and on them they all compete to have their cars on-line the cheapest. They show pictures and videos of the cars both new and used. They have pictures of all the employees, they want you to "like them on "facebook" or follow them on "twitter".

> **"But the tool the customer has that the dealer is most afraid of besides the factory survey is the "online review".**

This is where you can go onto "Google" or "Yahoo" or "Dealerater" or other sites and post reviews online about your experiences with a certain dealer. **If a dealer gets a bad review, it shows up on the internet.** Internet savvy customers today look at reviews for everything.

It will show how many stars out of 5 the review received. Enough bad reviews and the dealer will have a real problem.

At my last dealership we had a "social media manager" that only existed to manage the reviews we got on the internet. If we got a bad one, she tried to get it erased or contacted the customer to get it changed. **Dealers want as many "hits" on their websites as they can get.**

Also the mobile technology is rapidly changing the way cars are sold. It's common place now to see customers in the dealership looking online at their phones for the best price. **It has become a game changer.**

Chapter 14

Hybrids, Electric Cars & the Future.

A lot has been said recently in the automotive review magazines about how amazing the latest greatest hybrid car revolution has evolved. I myself have sold hybrid cars and electric cars.

The difference is the hybrid car runs off gasoline and electric batteries. The electric car runs totally on batteries, it has no engine and does not use gasoline.

The last manufacturer I worked for had both. **None of them sell.** Customers have not grasped the concept and are not willing to pay the extra price for the cars to offset the savings in not having to buy gas.

If model A comes in a gas version, and model A also comes in a hybrid version, the price for the hybrid can be $10,000 more. You have to drive a lot of miles without buying gas over many years to make up for that extra money you paid.

As we speak, the manufacturer that I last worked for had a totally electric car, but would only go 80 miles on a full charge. For around $2500 you can have a charging port built into your garage at home, or you can come to the dealership and charge the car.

This car never sold. The car is nicely equipped, some come with navigation and all the bells and whistles, and there is usually a hefty rebate or incentive when you buy or lease one of these cars, but I don't see it. **If you ever have to replace or repair the batteries forget about it.** These batteries are extremely expensive. And not just everyone can work on the car.

Some dealerships are not properly trained to repair these cars. But electric cars seem to be the hot topic. A company in California called "Tesla" makes a cool looking sports car that is fully electric, and goes about 200 miles on a full charge. Only problem is….the car cost around $70,000!

And with gas currently around 2.15 a gallon, you can buy a lot of car for that price and not miss the gas expense. And let's face it **the guy that can spend 70k for a car isn't worried about paying for gas anyway.** However many of these cars have been sold.

I recently was visiting a new "state of the art" shopping mall with my family. And right next to the Apple store, was a "Tesla" store. That's right; they had a car in the store, not just in the middle of the mall where you walk like a lot of dealers will place their cars for advertisement.

This was a store. You walked inside and there was a car. There was also a metal chassis with the batteries and motor assembled beside the car so you could see how the car was made. Salespersons walked around in the store with "ipads", and on the walls were all the color combinations and trim levels. You could pick from many different interior leather combinations and basically design the car exactly the way you want.

Obviously, I was intrigued and after sitting in the car and checking out all the cool technology, (the dash looked like a giant one touch computer screen) I started asking the salesperson (a nice looking young girl that didn't look like she could see a drowning man a life vest) "how all this works".

She politely informed me that here at the store you put in your "order" for the car, and then several months later you would receive instructions to pick up your car at the closet "delivery outlet".

No dealership, no showroom, no middle man, you are literally buying this car direct from the factory. Completely non negotiable, non confrontational, no managers lurking, no finance office, (I guess you provide your own financing). **"Tesla" has removed the dealer completely you are buying directly from the manufacturer**. It's an interesting concept.

Now this process has raised some eyebrows amongst dealers in this country, **because they don't like the prospect of customer's buying direct from the**

manufacturer, most states like Florida have concrete legislation that protects the dealer from this ever happening so we will have to see how the success of this "Tesla" concept plays out.

Today on the radio, I heard the Apple Computer Company is looking into producing a "self driven" car by 2020 called the "iCar". This also would be interesting to say in the least.

Technology with cars has come a long way. **Next year the government will make it standard equipment to put "back up cameras" in every car made. It won't be an option but a requirement.** New cars made today have lane changing warning systems that alert the driver when he is moving into a lane where another car is.

Cars are being made that stop or slow themselves down when an object is in front of them. It's really an exciting time for the automobile industry. Sales have not been higher than since before the "great recession" in 2008.

"Dealers are making more money than ever. Profits are reaching record levels".

Recently there has been the arrival of the "dealer conglomerate", these are publically traded companies like Autonation, that are buying up dealerships from "mom and pop" stores all over the country. They have corporate procedures in place and every store has the same processes.

Carmax is a huge used car player in the American market, opening up stores all over the country. I recently visited one and was "shocked" at the "laid back" mentality that the store operated under. All the employees dressed in shorts and tennis shoes. They specialize in only selling used cars. **No new cars. So their big business is trying to buy cars off the street.** I took my daughters car up there to see how this worked.

After about an hour wait, they went out and checked out her car, and came back with an amount they would pay me on the spot for her car. The offer was good for 7 days.

All I had to do was come in and produce the title, and they would cut me a check. Obviously, I knew exactly what her car was worth, and they tried to "low ball" me on their offer. I was told there was no negotiating allowed and the offer was final.

They didn't even try to sell me one of their cars! I was amazed. **At my dealership, we would have dragged the customer out in the hot sun and showed him 50 cars until the poor fellow said "ok, I like this one".**

So the business is changing, but keep in mind no matter what they do or say, or how nice they dress or what they wear, next time you go into a dealership, look around.

Notice all the expense it must take to run a large dealership every month.

All the employees have to be paid. All the vendors have to be paid. **Most dealerships have at least 10 million dollars just in cars on the ground.**

"Don't lose sight of the fact that they have are there to make money!"

Recently in the news, Warren Buffet's company Berkshire Hathaway, purchased a dealership conglomerate that operates many dealerships in America and he is one of the smartest and wealthiest people in the world! Why would he do that? **Because he knows they make money.**

Dealerships close or go out of business every day in this country. I know of a dealer that sold 500 cars a month and went bankrupt. It's not how many they sell its how much they make!

I remember a dealer telling me that when he goes to the bank they don't ask him how many cars he sold, they only ask HOW MUCH was he depositing!

Let them make their money........ **just don't let them make it all off of you.**

Chapter 15

My Story

I didn't wake up as a child and look around and say "wow mom and dad, I want to sell cars one day!" Actually I got into the car business by accident.

After going to college in California, I came home to the small town where my parents lived, and simply went to the nearest unemployment agency. They asked me some questions and I was asked if I ever considered sales, or selling cars.

I figured how bad could it be? I was dead broke driving a $500 car. After a couple days of training (which meant following some guy around while he sold cars) I was turned loose. **I sold 23 cars the first month.** I was salesmen of the month.

I made around $10,000 that first month and they gave me a brand new demo to drive at no charge! I thought I had hit the lottery. I'm barely 20 years old and in one month I had a pocket full of money, and a new car.

The next month I sold 31 cars and pocketed $14,000. Keep in **mind the average car salesperson in America sells about 10 cars a month**. Within, 6 months I was promoted to finance manager. Needless to say, I never went back to college.

By the time I was 29, I was a **General Manager** of a Multi-franchise new car dealership. I've was told at the time **I was one of the youngest General Managers in the country.** I continued over the years and up unto recently I was General Manager of 2 metro market new car franchises at the same time.

I have held every management position there is in the dealership except for service. I have trained hundreds of salespeople, tons of managers, and even **taught Dealers** how to make money in difficult times. My specialty was taking dealerships that were underperforming, and making them profitable in the shortest time possible.

Believe me when I say, **"this book you are reading is the finest and most comprehensive eye opening revelation about the car business there is out there".** I recently went to a large "big box" book store to see what other books were out there showing people how to "buy a car and save money". You know how many I found? None. Not one.

There were shelves and shelves on how to fix cars, and how to spot exotic cars, and how to paint cars etc...But not ONE BOOK on how to save money on the 2nd largest purchase you are ever going to make.

"If you only use ONE strategy in this book, it will more than pay for the cost of this book".

Also, I believe many people are intrigued about what really happens at a dealership, seeing behind the curtain, they want to see the "wizard". **"This book takes you where no one has gone before".**

I was recently at my son's baseball game. I was still running a couple of dealerships, and one of the dads came up to me and said, Jackson, so how does it really work? **"How do you guys get over on people"?**

At the time **I was actually insulted by the question.** What if I went over to the attorney watching his son's game and asked him that question?

But it got me to thinking. People really are curious about the inner workings of the car business, even if they are not buying a car. **And 99% of all the buyers out there have no idea what goes on,** how the money is made, and so on.

They have no idea how much money I made, or my manager's incomes. We look at credit applications every day. The average person in this country makes around $30,000 per year. That's a decent month for a General Manager. Why do they make so much? **Because, they generate millions of dollars in profits for the dealer.**

This book is the best representation of that. I promise you this; **if you read this book, and use the strategies** I have taught, and **don't save a minimum of $1000, simply write**

me a personal letter or email and I will refund the price you paid for this book. It doesn't get any better that that!

As I am writing this book I can't help to reflect on all the friends I have made over the years and worked with, and no doubt they will be disappointed that I wrote this book. **But this book was the culmination of years of knowledge and observation.**

You may find a column written about how to buy a car online or in a magazine, or some lack luster book on how to buy a car by some disgruntled ex salesman, but you will not find a book on the subject as detailed as mine. This book contains over 25 years of hands on experience in all facets of the buying experience.

"I showed dealers how make money, now I want to show you how to save it".

A wise man once said, **"The two days that are the most important in your life are the day you are born, and the day you realize WHY you were born".**

The End

Made in the USA
Columbia, SC
03 May 2023

16063859R00117